*Environmental Ethics
and the
Global Marketplace*

W9-CDA-836

WITHDRAWN

M.N. KEITH LIBRARY

Environmental Ethics and the Global Marketplace

EDITED BY

Dorinda G. Dallmeyer
and Albert F. Ike

The University of Georgia Press

Athens and London

137885

© 1998 by the University of Georgia Press
Athens, Georgia 30602
All rights reserved
Set in Sabon by G&S Typesetters, Inc.
Printed and bound by Braun-Brumfield, Inc.
The paper in this book meets the guidelines for
permanence and durability of the Committee on
Production Guidelines for Book Longevity of the
Council on Library Resources.

Printed in the United States of America

02 01 00 99 98   C   5 4 3 2 1

02 01 00 99 98   P   5 4 3 2 1

Library of Congress Cataloging in Publication Data

Environmental ethics and the global marketplace / edited by
    Dorinda G. Dallmeyer and Albert F. Ike.
        p.   cm.
    Includes bibliographical references and index.
    ISBN 0-8203-2003-X (alk. paper). — ISBN 0-8203-2015-3
(pbk. : alk. paper)
    1. Industrial management—Environmental aspects.
    2. Environmental ethics.   I. Dallmeyer, Dorinda G.
II. Ike, Albert F.
HD30.255.E578   1998
658.4'08—dc21   98-10309

British Library Cataloging in Publication Data available

Contents

Foreword

Andrew Young

I have always held that we are not going to be able to deal with our domestic economic difficulties, whatever they may be, until we reach out and include the whole globe. It is basically a zero-sum game. If the world in which we are doing business includes only Europe, North America, Japan, and the Pacific Rim, we will end up in varieties of cut-throat competition and protectionism or trade wars, however subtle or overt, that nobody can ever win. The tragedy is that we are wasting this kind of intellectual energy when nearly 70 percent of the world needs and wants everything we know how to do.

Let me give an example. With adequate fresh water in West Africa, you can wipe out forty-one diseases, even without medicines. We know about water. We know how to find it, purify it, desalt it, and transport it safely. There is water available everywhere on the face of this earth. We know how to provide water, and yet we have not provided water. If we decide to provide every human being on the face of the earth access to clean, pure water, think of the work that it would require. It would require piping; it would require engineering services, it would require an understanding of water resources management; it would require trucks; it would require putting citizens of the world to work—just on providing water. We tend not to think big anymore. But those of us who grew up in the Southeast and who are about my age can remember when this was a difficult and very barren area. It was the Tennessee Valley Authority and government involvement in creating man-made lakes, building roads, extending rural electric lines, and planting pine trees which played an extremely important role in sustaining, protecting, and preserving the beautiful environment we now enjoy. I have ridden a bicycle from north Georgia down to Savannah. There is probably no more beautiful part of the world than the environment in north Georgia, but it is essentially an environment that has been preserved, protected, rescued, you might say, from the ravages of the last century. It was a sense of responsibility not just to the earth but also to people that led to Georgia's revitalization.

On a recent trip to Warm Springs, Georgia, we admired all of the trees that President Franklin Delano Roosevelt planted. The Pine Mountain trail, and all that beauty we now protect and preserve around Callaway Gardens, essentially was a product of people who really loved the land but, more important, loved the people who lived on the land. Although it might be rejected today as a big government boondoggle, FDR's New Deal gave hope to poor, starving, anguished people in this region. These are the kinds of efforts that made America great. With all of the faults and mistakes that we have made environmentally in Georgia, if you weigh us in the balance and determine what has happened here, what we have done has benefited almost all of the people involved. That is the way I approach the questions of environmental ethics.

Religiously, I say that the earth is the Lord's. I also have to say that all of these creations, whether the birds of the air or the beasts of the field (including human beings), are part of an environment that we are responsible for preserving and protecting. It seems to me that the ethics of the environment essentially is the stewardship of the resources with which God has entrusted us. If we love ourselves and anybody else, we have to make sure that this environment is enhanced rather than destroyed.

Now, rather than limit our focus to trees or endangered species, let us also consider the part of the globe within our midst that we too often ignore. There is, in the midst of the United States, a $400 billion economy, larger than Mexico and Canada put together, and yet we have relatively weak environmental protection laws in effect. We don't share equally in the resources of the land on which we live, and that problem is threatening to destroy the lives of the rest of us. The endangered species that would populate this economy about which I am speaking is the black male, the unemployed, undereducated black male who right now is being relegated more frequently to prison than to college, and that in itself is destructive of the total environment. It makes no sense for a society to spend $25,000 a year to put somebody in jail when you can send that person to college for $5,000.

Let me suggest an environmentally sound method of coping with this problem, which also happens to be very good business. The Music Corporation of America (MCA) was looking at Atlanta as a site for some kind of amphitheater for their big rock concerts. Nobody really wanted them in Chastain Park and nobody wanted them in anybody's neighborhood. They were going so far north of Atlanta, around Alpharetta, that they were afraid that nobody would come. The costs of building roads and using the resources out there would have been destructive to one of the most beautiful parts of our county. We finally persuaded MCA to let us help them to locate down at the old Lakewood Fairgrounds. What we did was go into the community, talk to the young men who were unemployed, give them an opportunity not only to be employed but to run a business. We formed young men into a security company and created a joint venture partnership with another company responsible for the security of the area. Not a single piece of material was stolen from the job site. MCA said they built amphitheaters all over the county—all over the world—and they had never had a situation where they lost absolutely nothing in construction. But the contractor who was doing it also grew up near that community, and he recruited additional people from the neighborhood to work there. The women, many of whom were on or just off welfare or unemployed, were formed into a concessions company. They were given 35 percent ownership of the hot dog stands, the popcorn, and the food concessions. The older men, many of whom had not worked in years, formed a parking lot company. They received 35 percent of the contract to run the parking.

The end result is that MCA got a facility right on an intersection of

I-75/85 and 166, a prime location. The only thing wrong with that location was that it was filled with poor people who happened to be black. But we brought some money in and we gave the people in the community an opportunity for ownership. When we made it possible for people in a capitalistic economy to have access to capital, it worked. That facility has been functioning there for ten years. Cars don't get stolen. They haven't had any gang fights. Utilizing all of the resources of that community and the financial resources in a free market environment, in which the ethics of that environment required a fair opportunity not just for work but for ownership and participation in the growth and development of the neighborhood, it worked. It worked and it is beginning to stimulate other good things as a result. People have steady jobs and own part of a business. The city's role was to provide accountants and business consultants to nurse the economic process along.

My contention is that whenever we set out to develop the economy and the quality of life of the total community, if we think of the earth as the Lord's and everybody being a child of God to share equally in access to opportunity and blessing, the environment can be protected and preserved. When we want to take shortcuts, when we want to get a little more than our share, it backfires. Looking at that model on a global basis, we have more than a theoretical ethic of success. We have real models to use as guides to action.

I have been asked by President Clinton to help in South Africa with an enterprise development fund. South Africa is an incredible opportunity. One of the first things we have hit upon is how you generate wealth. If you generate wealth and respect, the people who are generating and producing the wealth will protect their environment. We started with a group of market women, working with beads, sitting on the ground. They will string beads all day long and probably sell them for fifteen cents or a quarter, or if they catch tourists coming through, maybe one dollar. Somebody got the idea that, given the skill and talent and the artistic ability of these women working with beads, what would happen if they were doing the same thing with diamonds, pearls, gold or semiprecious stones? All of these resources are right there in the earth in South Africa. So we set up a project to use a little bit of our money to create the opportunity to help these women learn to cut and polish diamonds and work with gold. Instead of working all day and getting a dollar for their work, by doing the same amount of work and using the same amount of creative artistic ability with gold, diamonds, and platinum, they will probably be able to earn $10,000 for that project. We are not giving them the $10,000; we are loaning them the raw materials and allowing them to turn it into something that we might consider precious. All of a sudden you find that you are using the earth's resources that have been taken for granted and you are generating wealth. First of all, people who stop selling beads for a dollar and start selling gold and diamonds for thousands of dollars will send all their children to college. They will provide health care for themselves. They will begin to build homes. But they will also want to purchase some of the products. They will contribute to the global economy.

One of our most successful projects in Nigeria took me only about twenty minutes to put together when I was ambassador. They were wasting natural gas by flaring it off as we did in the Gulf of Mexico for years. They also were importing $90 million of fertilizer a year. I told them we knew how to convert natural gas to fertilizer, but for the Nigerians the U.S. company's price was too high. The Europeans' prices were $30–40 million cheaper, and the Japanese were charging about $50 million less. But the U.S. firm happened to be a *Texas* firm. I knew there were a lot of Nigerians studying at the University of Houston. So I suggested to the Nigerian president that if he would sign with this Texas company and put as a component of the deal that they train Nigerian engineers to manage the project when it was complete, I thought we could make a deal. Not only would he get a project that would turn wasted gas into fertilizer to grow crops, but he would also have a workforce that would know how to run the plant. Now that plant is running as a $400 million operation with five hundred Nigerian workers trained in the southern part of the United States as co-op students working in American plants, and it didn't cost anybody anything. Everybody won. Nigerians are no longer wasting natural gas; they are no longer importing fertilizer; they are exporting it. Almost any time we decide that we want to make the world make sense, we have the technology and the wealth to do it. If we love the earth and know that the earth is the Lord's and that the people dwell therein as brothers and sisters, we can create the kind of environment that will not only preserve and protect the planet but will do so at a profit! I think that the key to capitalism that we miss all the time is if you do good, you can do well.

It may have been a humanitarian decision that made Robert W. Woodruff say that anywhere in the world an American soldier goes, we are going to see to it that he gets a Coca-Cola. That was the kind of decision that contributed to Coca-Cola's 22 percent rise in profits in 1994. They became a global company by going with the troops and deciding that Coca-Cola ought to be everywhere. This approach to marketing may not seem very important in the grand scheme of things, but Coca-Cola is the fourth largest employer in South Africa. It provides, and that is what the Bible says. You are supposed to feed the hungry, clothe the naked, and heal the sick. People who work for Coca-Cola eat. They send their children to school. They generate wealth. God's world makes sense. We have the kingdom in our midst if we are ethically sensitive and if we realize that this is not our planet. It belongs not to us but to generations yet unborn.

One of the American Indian leaders who visited me at the United Nations sternly reminded me that in their nations you don't make decisions just for yourself or just for your children. Your decisions have to be made for seven generations yet unborn. If we look at this planet and make decisions for seven generations yet unborn, we will resolve economic conflicts. We will somehow resolve the ethnic differences to the point where we appreciate diversity rather than being threatened by it. We will move into the twenty-first century with the kind of confidence and vision that will make this a good place to be for seven generations yet unborn.

Preface

The global market is the largest and most powerful socioeconomic institution on the planet, and as such it demands that those who desire to benefit from it or those who seek to regulate it must realize the economic and environmental consequences of their actions. The UN Conference on Environment and Development, held in Rio de Janeiro in 1992, highlighted the intersection of the interests of international commerce and environmental ethicists. These interests coincide or conflict as international trade expands and global environmental deterioration becomes more serious. Judging from the range of arguments heard concerning the provisions of the General Agreement on Tariffs and Trade (GATT), the likely effects of the North American Free Trade Agreement (NAFTA), and the potential long-range implications of the 1992 Rio Conference, there is little likelihood any time soon of spontaneous agreement among economists, environmentalists, and corporate representatives regarding criteria for an economically responsible approach to a unified set of international environmental policies. The interests and aims of these different groups often seem diametrically opposed. Some people, however, maintain that this apparent divergence of interest is an illusion.

Two important considerations dictate that economic health and the preservation of environmental values cannot long diverge. First, there is ample evidence showing that the health of the environment is inextricably linked to the health of the economy, and appropriate environmental legislation is politically achievable only in a context of overall economic strength. Just as chronic poverty invariably results in environmental devastation, environmental protection efforts are self-defeating, politically impossible, and ethically indefensible if they substantially undermine the economic conditions that make such protection feasible. Second, economic strength depends on the preservation of environmental values. A stable economy requires conservation of the natural systems on which we depend for both trade and sustenance. Ultimately, economic and environmental sciences must merge more completely if we are to arrive at ethically justified principles as the basis for national and international environmental policy.

In a recent article, Capra and Mager state, "Because of its pursuit of unrestricted economic growth, business has been the main driving force of global environmental deterioration. . . . Yet because it is so powerful, business can also be an important agent of change." In the United States, many corporations over the last decade have instituted internal changes to make their operations more ecologically sound. While the intersection of the interests of environmental ethicists and international business persons was highlighted by the 1992 Rio Conference, it will be years before the ideas generated there are common practice around the world. Because of their worldwide reach, multinational corporations have the opportunity to institute environmentally responsible management practices in advance of global regulatory efforts.

This book is a compilation of papers presented at the 1995 conference "Environmental Ethics and the Global Marketplace," held at the University of Georgia. The conference was designed to provide a state-of-the-art forum where academic theorists from the fields of environmental ethics, law, and science could meet with international corporate leaders to craft a synthesis on how to deal with a common problem: to enlarge the entire concept of management to create sustainable business practices that work in harmony with the environment instead of at its expense. In this multidisciplinary forum, theorists were able to test practice and practitioners to test theory, to find areas of agreement and disagreement, and to see that all interests are represented in the process of developing international economic and environmental regulations. Finding common ground was not easily achieved. Those authors contributing to this book often did not agree with each other.

The goal of this book is to focus on the divergence of interest and opinion concerning environmental and economic goals. Environmental ethicists and business executives seldom, if ever, jointly discuss global trends and seek a common purpose. Rather, the interaction between environmentalists and commercial interests is mediated by a complex of culture, history, technology, and law. Our purpose is to bridge this complexity and create a dialogue between those who focus on international commerce and those concerned with the ethical grounds for managing the global environment. It was our aim to provide a forum within which world experts from a variety of fields and backgrounds could discuss the relationship between environmental and economic values, and move toward an economically and environmentally informed consensus on the criteria for responsible policy choice.

The book opens with an examination of the interactions among environmental ethics, the global marketplace, and areas of conflict that stand in the way of achieving consensus. To set the stage Frederick Ferré poses several questions: Who are we? Where did we come from? Where are we going? and What does it matter? "We" are from a variety of professions, agencies, governmental units, and nongovernmental organizations (NGOs) gathered to reflect on our role of being ethical agents. We come from various localities and walks of life. Where we are going depends on our readiness to listen attentively and to speak frankly from our respective experiences and expertise on issues of concern in environmental ethics and the global economy; namely, what shall we value? We are here to place the global marketplace within the larger context of facts and values. The answer to the question "What does it matter?" is crucial.

Humans require clean air, fresh water, and adequate food for continued survival. Judith L. Meyer focuses on these aspects of the global environment. Human activity is altering global cycles of carbon and nitrogen with far-reaching impacts on our air and water. Freshwaters have been highly altered by human activity. Increasing numbers of countries experience water stress, and fisheries have been destroyed. Salinization resulting from poor irrigation practices, accelerating rates of soil erosion, reduced effectiveness of pesticides and fertilizers, and loss of arable land to cities have all had a negative impact on global food production. Humans are altering the global environment because of their rapid rate of population increase and accelerating resource consumption. The limit to the number of people this planet can support is determined by the availability of resources and the amount of resources required by each human. Humans currently appropriate over 40 percent of all terrestrial primary productivity and thereby reduce the resources available to other species. Meyer argues that humans are a part of the web of life on the planet and they have a moral obligation to help maintain that web. How large a proportion of our earth's resources should a morally responsible human be consuming?

Despite a twenty-year history as a subdiscipline within philosophy, environmental ethics remains an esoteric field with little influence in environmental affairs. In the view of Eugene Hargrove, the chief problem is that environmental professionals continue to be trained to be objective and value-free, which essentially inoculates them against values and ethics education. Although this training is a blend of three recent ethical positions—utilitarianism, pragmatism, and logical positivism or emotivism—it is presented as a factual position that is completely independent of philosophy. This training is incompatible with the spirit, if not the letter, of our environmental laws. These processes of redefinition function as a kind of environmental "Newspeak" that prevents environmental professionals from being able to think in accordance with our socially evolved values and ideals. Such influences make it impossible for these professionals to carry out our environmental laws as they were originally written. As environmental "Newspeak," this process is undermining the valuational framework that defines what we stand for as a nation and threatens to make our common heritage unintelligible.

The book then turns to the regulatory system and the challenges facing it. Environmentalists often offer prudential arguments for restraining economic growth. They believe that the global economy, by depleting natural resources and overburdening sinks for wastes, exceeds the carrying capacity of the earth. Those who promote economic growth counter that the carrying capacity of the earth is a function of technology. As a result of advances in knowledge, resources are becoming ever more plentiful, commodity and food prices are falling, and where wealth increases so does air, water, and environmental quality. Mark Sagoff argues that controversies about carrying capacity and the sustainability of economic growth obscure more pressing moral issues concerning our obligation to the intrinsic (as distinct from the instrumental) qualities of nature. In other words, the demise of wildlife, the loss of natural ecosystems, and the destruction of our ecological and evolutionary heritage should concern us even if technology can create a "second nature" economically more valuable or more efficient than the original nature that it is replacing everywhere.

Faced with unparalleled environmental constraints, a number of constituencies, including business, government, and environmental organizations, are encouraging business schools to develop visions for a "new and improved" business curriculum. These developmental efforts (both in traditional and nontraditional academic settings) attempt to integrate some implications of current world environmental conditions into business curricula and aim at replacing the "business as usual" paradigm with a significantly different worldview. This, in turn, necessitates the incorporation of dimensions previously not included in traditional business education. Jan Willem Bol identifies some of these developmental efforts and examines the rate with which these curricular innovations are being adopted by schools of business.

It is widely recognized that moral ideas motivate people to care for the world around them, but how do values and value changes translate into policies, decisions, and behavior that will move the world toward sustainability? Changing public attitudes will be important in the long run, but what will have a *direct and immediate impact* is making careful articulation of value choices an explicit part of decision making. The five-year program outlined by Thaddeus Trzyna will work systematically to build ethics into the decision-making processes of organizations whose international activities have an important influence on sustainable development. This program represents a refocusing and expansion of work that started fifteen years ago under the auspices of the World Conservation Union (IUCN). It is operated by a small international consortium of NGOs and an expanded IUCN Ethics Working Group, in cooperation with the IUCN Secretariat.

The collection then turns to the links between theory and ethics. While there is a wide range of supporting evidence that environmental problems exist for minorities and low-income populations, much of the evidence claimed to support or show racial discrimination consists of case studies or analyses that may lack sufficient empirical rigor to establish affirmative evidence of discrimination based on race. Warren Kriesel and Terence J. Centner present analyses of pollution and siting data to discern whether there exists evidence of environmental injustice. The first analysis considers differential exposure to ambient pollutants by examining toxic release data. From the analysis of 645 Georgia zip code areas, it is possible to show that race matters more than income in determining burdens of released toxic materials, but the racial effect is very sensitive to how income is specified in the model. The second analysis involves the targeting of minority and poor communities for undesirable land uses. Using an industrial location model, the analysis shows no evidence that potentially polluting manufacturers are attracted to poor Georgia counties or to counties with proportionately higher nonwhite populations. Rather, standard location factors such as transportation access and infrastructure have a greater impact on location decisions. While their chapter focuses on environmental justice issues only in a domestic U.S. context, Kriesel and Centner's concluding discussion of environmental equity suggests intriguing consequences were it to be applied internationally.

Science and technology cannot foresee every possible consequence of human actions in the environment. Hans Jonas, in his *Imperative of Responsibility* (1984), argues convincingly that an "imperative of responsibility" in environmental and technological ethics emerges from the problem of prediction. Holmes Rolston offers a similar argument in his 1988 *Environmental Ethics*, maintaining that actions in the environment, such as the use of a new pesticide, must be considered suspect until proven otherwise. However, in William J. McKinney's discussion of the nature of thought experiments (the tool that Jonas argues must be employed in order to act ethically in the environment), McKinney discusses a weakness in both Jonas's and Rolston's positions. Thought experiments suffer from the same predictive difficulties as experiments in the physical and social worlds, and can be shown to depend on experiments in the external world for their very existence. Thus, a return to Jonas's purely contemplative science is quite impossible, both ethically and scientifically.

Markku Oksanen focuses on the relationship between property rights and environmental conservation. His main target is Robert Goodin's analysis of the concept of ownership, which Oksanen characterizes as narrow. Does it also miss the idea of how ownership is commonly under-

stood? On the other hand, if we accept Blackstone's strong, if not absolutist, concept of ownership, is it at odds with environmentalist objectives?
Oksanen also considers issues related to the application of general and
universal definitions to social and legal concepts.

The book then addresses the intersection of economics and ethics. In
David Skrbina's view, the approval of NAFTA and the World Trade Organization by the U.S. government seriously undermines efforts in moving society toward environmental sustainability. The very process of free
trade leads to accelerated resource depletion, absentee ownership and loss
of local control, and the disempowering of people everywhere. Accountability is moving into the hands of international corporations that may be
driven to unethical practices by factors beyond their control. Because free
trade manifests itself as orienting economies toward greater consumption
of imports and greater production of exports, Skrbina concludes that
the rational and ethical course of action is to reduce both imports and
exports.

Conflicts over forests and forest resources have garnered attention in
the tropics, the U.S. Pacific Northwest, and British Columbia's Clayoquot
Sound. Doug Daigle views these conflicts not as isolated incidents but as
part of a far larger process: the globalization of the timber trade. This process manifests itself in trends that are transforming the timber industry,
such as a shift of industry focus from tropical to temperate and boreal
forests, the surging growth of the world pulp and paper market, and increasing centralization of the timber industry into a smaller and smaller
number of large transnational corporations. Each of these trends has significant implications for the world's forests. But there are also fundamentally flawed assumptions underlying most government policies about forest use. Two prominent ones are the undervaluation of forests, in which
forests have no value until they are logged and commodified, and the ex-
aggeration of the benefits of industrial logging, usually a means of providing rural employment. Daigle challenges both of these assumptions and
points out how a number of alternative models of forests valuation and
resource use have been articulated.

The book concludes with a consensus statement of recommendations
generated by speakers and participants at the conference. In the summary,
the group identifies the need for a theoretical basis to underpin an ethical

framework capable of addressing the social costs and benefits of the policy process. By establishing linkages systematically to bring ethical considerations into the policy process, it would be possible to move environmental ethics beyond academic venues into domestic and international decision making.

Acknowledgments

The editors wish to express their deep appreciation to other members of the organizing committee for the conference that gave rise to this volume. Planning support was provided by Asterios Kefelas, professor of organizational management in the Terry College of Business, and by Frank Golley, past chair of the faculty of the Environmental Ethics Certificate Program at the University of Georgia. Golley also represented the Institute of Ecology, which has recently expanded its program of interdisciplinary studies to involve subjects in the social sciences and humanities, particularly in conservation ecology, sustainable development, and anthropology. Clark Wolf, an environmental ethicist in the Department of Philosophy, and Richard C. Field, public service associate at the Georgia Center for Continuing Education, participated in planning the conference, as did Andrew Keeler and Terry Centner of the Department of Agriculture and Applied Economics, who joined the planning committee in September 1994.

We wish to thank the following units of the University of Georgia for their sponsorship of the conference: the Environmental Ethics Certificate Program, the Dean Rusk Center for International and Comparative Law, the Institute of Ecology, the Humanities Center, and the Office of International Development. We are grateful for a state-of-the-art conference grant from the office of the vice president for academic affairs, which provided the primary financial foundation for the conference.

We also wish to thank the corporate sponsors of the conference—Georgia-Pacific, the Georgia Power Company, the Law Companies, R.E.M./Athens L.L.C., and Southwire Company—whose financial support enabled us to concentrate on the quality and substance of the conference itself. Special thanks is extended to Margaret Caufield, conference coordinator at the Georgia Center for Continuing Education.

*Environmental Ethics
and the
Global Marketplace*

FREDERICK FERRÉ

Where Are We Going?

A Statement of the Problem

The editors of this volume have handed the opening statement of the problem to me, a philosopher. We philosophers are the ones who are always stuck with grand problems: Who are we? Where do we come from? Where are we going? Why does it matter?

All right. I surrender to my role. Who are "we," the readers of this book, supposed to be? This is a question, if we keep it limited, with a definite answer. In addition to teachers, students, and concerned citizens, "we" are government officials, lawyers, environmental consultants, scientists, corporate policymakers from national and multinational institutions, leaders of nongovernmental environmental organizations—and we are all ethical agents whether we like it or not (displaying our ethics in our practices if not in our professions). A few of us are also philosophers, reflecting on ethics as best we can.

Where do we come from? Here is another answerable question, if we don't push it too far. "We," who for one reason or another have chosen to start reading this book, will come from many places around this globe. Many of us will be local, relative to the editors and press—American citizens now living through the twitching tail-end of the second millennium of this Common Era. But all of us, no matter how far distant from American shores, are "local" somewhere: namely, where the rubber of the human chariot hits the hard environmental road that unites us all.

Where are we going? For answers I must summarize the aim of the book as a whole. This volume has a purpose. It is to challenge persons from different realities—from disparate localities and professional worlds. It is not usual, not easy, to find corporate policymakers stating their ideas on the environment in direct juxtaposition with researchers fresh from the field or laboratory (or vice versa), or for lawyers and ethical theorists to tangle with all of the above—all bound together under a common cover. Businessmen and scholars, government officials and nongovernmental activists, will meet in the following chapters without intermediaries. They share visions of the world, concerns, worries, and hopes, without the usual compartmentalization (and distortion) with which our overspecialized society is all too familiar.

This heady pluralism is something that some (though unfortunately few) academics have come to appreciate. But it has taken effort. At complex "multiversities," faculty members have to overcome significant levels of suspicion at the very idea of interdisciplinary work in environmental ethics. Still, environmental studies by their very nature require the pooling of expertise from many disciplines. Anyone who has attempted serious work in the area knows that the conditions seem impossibly diverse. But, despite this, programs of this sort are thriving at a number of institutions, and their participants—faculty and students alike—have found them vital avenues for face-to-face, unmediated conversations of high intellectual caliber among people who would never otherwise have met, far less shared with each other their mutual concerns about the environment and values. I personally am one who has learned to enjoy the excitement of this sort of academic adventure outside the safe bounds of my own specialties.

Not just "to enjoy." To need! Now that I have come to realize what a difference to my thinking it makes to be brought up short in the middle of an "obvious" point by another respected colleague who doesn't see things from the same angle at all, I can hardly imagine plunging back into my old disciplinary tunnel. Students feel the same way, sometimes risking peril with the "powers that be" in their home departments as a result. But such students, standing at the cusp of the new millennium in which they will spend most of their productive lives, rightly see that the most important issues are not single-discipline problems. To do the needed ecological work on global warming (to take just one example), the knowledge of specialists in atmospheric science, chemistry, physics, geology, meteorology, microbiology, soils, and more must be harnessed together if we are to understand what global warming or ozone depletion may mean in factual terms. And that is just the beginning! We need simultaneously to know what human decisions have resulted in interventions by Homo sapiens into the global atmosphere, and how human beings organize themselves into societies that wage high-tech wars or form mega-institutions such as the global marketplace. If they are destructive to the long-term well-being of humans and the earth's life system, how are human actions to be modified? Can human beings respond to rational argument, or must we be manipulated by levers of fear (real or imagined) or lures of greed? Who are we? Where have we come from? Where are we going? To answer these questions in this new, larger—and more urgent—context requires the best insights of economics and sociology, of psychology, anthropology, history, and—yes—of philosophy, theology, and ethics.

Returning to the topic of ethics leads me to make a final philosopher's point about the problem of this book. We have one shared problem, deep beneath and far above all our many differences. The problem, forced on us as fellow human beings tied together in the inescapable role of ethical agents, is this: What shall we value? All life is valuing. This need not (usually does not) imply consciousness of preference, but all living creatures show preferences (positive and negative) if only through their behavior. Even as the lowly amoeba reaches out its tiny pseudopodia for nourishment, and even as the gazelle runs from the pursuing cheetah (here both negative and positive values are acted out), so the entrepreneur reaches out for profit; the scientist, for discovery; the lawyer, for a favorable verdict. Were we not motivated by preferences and aversions, we would quickly die as individuals and as a species.

What is striking about the human species is that our preferences and our aversions are to a large extent conscious, or at least capable of being brought to conscious awareness—and therefore open to critical examination. What at first we may be inclined to value might, on second thought, be found harmful to us in the long run. One of the special capacities of Homo sapiens is to be able to defer immediate gratifications for the sake of greater goods to be harvested in the future. We are a form of living organism capable of elaborating priorities of preferences, organizing value systems. We are animals who can feel moral obligation, who can experience shame at injustice, who can subordinate inclination to duty. Not all members of our species are equally adept at conscious value-criticism and preference-ordering. Indeed, most ordinary folk spend precious little time examining personal values on their own. But ethical codes and religious systems, developed by some in society for the well-being (in principle and intention) of all in society, give group guidance for normal situations encountered over the millennia of human experience, even where private ethical thinking is sluggish or dim.

The problem of this book, however, is that what has been "normal" for human experience over the millennia is now crumbling before our eyes. And, alas, the eyes of most ordinary inhabitants of this radically changing world have not been picking up on the changes. It takes special effort, training, and concentration to become critically aware of the new facts in their complexity and subtlety; likewise, it takes special effort, training, and concentration to consider critically what these new facts mean for modifications of human value systems and preference priorities adequate to the new millennium.

We correctly note with awe that one of the foci of this book's discussion, the global market, is the world's largest institution. It is impossible to overstate its importance in shaping our present and future. But we should also confess, with some humility, that the other two foci of this volume, the environment and ethics, are larger yet. Neither count as institutions, but it is only thanks to the resources and constraints of the natural environment and only because of the pervasive motivations of human preferences and value schemes—including duties and obligations—that all institutions, including the global market, are formed and sustained and reformed.

We need to understand the global marketplace in this larger context of facts and values. We need to triangulate toward our future—where we are going—with clear sightings from each point. Therefore, we need to pay attention to each author as each writes with special knowledge. But our relationship to values is somewhat different from our relationship to the other standpoints. We are not all scientists; we are not all lawyers or NGO leaders; we are not all captains of corporate enterprises. But we are all human; therefore, we are all conscious valuers. And we are all under obligation as ethical agents to be as wisely conscious of our preference priorities and value systems as we possibly can be. Thinking sloppy ethical thoughts is a culpable ethical defect. We are derelict in our duties as humans, whatever else our roles may be, if we fail to use the special gifts of our species to bring our priorities and our attitudes into line with the realities we are creating with our actions on earth.

Here, then, are some of the really underlying problems to ponder in reading this book: What is it we are drawn to when we pursue goals within the global market? Is it profit? What is the fundamental good of profit? Is it creating wealth? What is the fundamental meaning of *wealth?* The word comes from *weal,* meaning well-being, as in the old word *commonweal* or, interchangeably, *commonwealth*. What is the common weal for humans? How many material things add up to "enough" for well-being? Does *enough* mean the same for every culture? Is there a level of weal below which no one should be required to live, whatever the culture? Does the global market have an effective way of addressing the issue of fair distribution of human weal? Do we have a moral obligation to humans yet unborn? Does the global market work for or against intergenerational justice? If we value such justice, can markets be made to work with greater consideration for generations who cannot themselves claim fair treatment from the present generation of humans?

And more: Is our species' weal the only well-being that counts? In the light of new factual understanding, do we need to adjust our priorities to include the weal of nonhuman creatures, the weal of the environment we have so long taken for granted as existing only to serve human weal? If so, should this readjustment in values be made simply to enlarge the concept of enlightened human self-interest—for example, to prevent future increases of skin cancer in humans, to avoid the inundation of island nations or coastal cities by rising ocean levels, to preserve the possibility of unknown medicines from creatures living in endangered rain forests, in other words, to escape collapse in our way of life—or should our values-scheme be altered to include direct concern for the weal of the land and its creatures for their own sake, not only for ours?

The values I have stressed so far are the practical values of physical well-being and the obligations of ethical fairness, but there are others we sometimes forget in our emphasis on the practical and the obligatory. These are the values of beauty and holiness. They deserve a place in our volume, too. Human weal is not measured in bread and duties alone, but also by intrinsic joys of aesthetic completion and by spiritual serenity in balance with the ultimate. How does the power of the global market relate to these?

I began with the questions, Who are we? Where did we come from? Where are we going?—and one more question, What does it matter? The first three are answered well enough for now, I hope. But the fourth, barely asked, is the key to it all. If anything at all matters, it does so only because we living beings are valuing beings. Things do matter to creatures like us. Our global ecosystem is currently under great stress. That matters. There is great maldistribution of wealth in the human world. That matters. The global market is the largest and most powerful institution on earth for dealing weal or woe to future generations and to the earth as a whole. Because all this really matters, "we," the readers, have picked up this book. It provides us a chance to gain ideas about how we can make a difference where it matters. Let the reading begin!

JUDITH L. MEYER

The Changing State
of the Global Environment

Homo sapiens, like other species on our planet, requires clean air, fresh water, and adequate food for continued survival. This chapter will focus on these aspects of our environment. The topic is the state of the global environment; however, rather than a static focus, I will emphasize the changing state of the global environment, for we live on a planet that is ever-changing. Knowing the current state of the environment is insufficient; we also must consider how and at what rate our planetary environment is changing (Meyer 1994).

Consider first the air that surrounds us. We know with certainty that the concentration of carbon dioxide in the atmosphere is increasing. Air bubbles trapped in Antarctic ice show that atmospheric CO_2 concentration is currently higher than it has been for the past 160,000 years (Barnola et al. 1987). This increase is a consequence of human activity. Concentrations of methane are also rising for the same reason (Vitousek 1994).

The effect of these changes on global climate has received widespread attention, so I will not discuss it here. Instead, I will focus on well-documented direct consequences of these increases in carbon dioxide on plants, for these have been overlooked in the contentious debate about climate change.

Plants increase their growth rate in response to increased CO_2, and species differ in the magnitude and sustainability of their response. Some species grow faster in the first year of exposure to elevated CO_2 but return to initial growth rates in subsequent years; other species grow less initially but then grow more rapidly in subsequent years (Bazzaz, Miao, and Wayne 1994). This differential growth response can alter the outcome of competition between different plant species, for example, between crops and weeds or between native species and introduced exotics (Smith, Strain, and Sharkey 1987).[1] Forests and fields with a changed species composition are one likely consequence of human alteration of the atmosphere.

Plants also respond to elevated CO_2 by producing tissue poorer in nitrogen (Bazzaz 1990). These changes in the chemistry of plant tissues alter the rate at which herbivorous insects consume plants, as well as altering insect mortality and reproduction (Fajer, Bowers, and Bazzaz 1989). In addition, it is likely that rates of decomposition will be altered because the amount of nitrogen in plant tissues influences their decay rate. Hence, this change in plant chemistry could alter the rates at which nitrogen is recycled back to the plant community (Norby, Pastor, and Melillo 1986).

Our earth's atmosphere is predominantly nitrogen, and the global nitrogen cycle has been altered markedly by human activity. Fixation of nitrogen by humans for fertilizers currently exceeds natural rates of nitrogen fixation and leads to excess deposition of biologically available nitrogen in terrestrial and aquatic environments (Vitousek 1994). This has resulted in increased loads of nitrate in aquatic environments correlated with the increase in nitrate fertilizer use (Turner and Robelais 1991).[2] Another well-documented consequence of high rates of fertilizer production is the excess deposition of nitrate in rainfall; this has been linked to forest dieback in Europe (Schultze 1989).

Humans have affected our atmosphere at both global (for example, stratospheric ozone hole) and local scales (for example, elevated ozone in metropolitan areas). These changes threaten the health of humans and other species. Changes in other aspects of our environment also threaten human health. Let us consider another of life's essentials: fresh water.

Clean water is a luxury that we in the developed world take for granted. Each day, 25,000 people on our planet die from water-borne diseases (Meybeck, Chapman, and Helmer 1989). Human health can be directly related to availability of safe drinking water. When one examines the rankings of countries with respect to child mortality, there is an inverse correlation between that statistic and the proportion of the population with access to safe drinking water (Engelman and LeRoy 1993).[3] Clean water is also a casualty of industrialization without environmental controls: three-fourths of Poland's river water is too contaminated for even industrial use (Postel 1992).

What can be accomplished with environmental controls? Consider the case of lead in the United States. With passage of the Clean Water Act and Clean Air Act in the 1970s and with consequent use of unleaded fuels, the amount of lead used in gasoline in the United States plummeted; at the same time, average levels of lead in human blood decreased (Meybeck, Chapman, and Helmer 1989).[4] Would car manufacturers have shifted to unleaded gas without the regulatory stimulus? It seems unlikely. Regulation levels the economic playing field so that all companies have to play by the same rules; this enables businesses to make changes that could otherwise put them at a competitive disadvantage.

Global water use is currently 4,340 km^3/yr, about eight times the annual discharge of the Mississippi River (Postel 1992). Human use of water has been increasing and is not evenly distributed around the globe. Water use has increased exponentially in Asia from 414 km^3/yr in 1900 to 2,440 km^3/yr in 1990 (Meybeck, Chapman, and Helmer 1989). In 1990, twenty-eight countries with a combined population of 232 million people experienced water stress; that is, annual available water was less than 1,000 m^3/person. The number of countries experiencing water stress is expected to double in the next thirty years (Postel 1992). To put this concept of water stress in some perspective, annual per capita water consumption in the United States is 1,863 m^3 (Raven, Berg, and Johnson 1995).[5]

Water is consumed directly by humans, but it also provides food in the form of fish and irrigated crops. Inland fisheries have been destroyed in many parts of the world. For example, in the Caspian Sea the 1990 commercial fish catch was less than 1 percent of the 1950 catch. The Aral Sea offers an even more dramatic example. The government of the former Soviet Union made a conscious decision to sacrifice an ecosystem the size of Ireland for increased economic benefits from irrigated agriculture. Since 1960, the area of the Aral Sea has decreased by 40 percent, its volume has decreased by 60 percent, its salinity has increased threefold, and twenty-four native fish species have disappeared (Postel 1992). The fish catch in the 1950s was on the order of 44,000 tons/yr; it is now zero.

Agriculture uses more water than any other human activity, so I will turn now to the third aspect of our environment that is essential for human survival: food. In the past four decades, we have seen dramatic increases in the global food supply, yet these trends are changing. Salinization resulting from poor irrigation practices, accelerating rates of soil erosion, reduced effectiveness of pesticides and fertilizers, and loss of arable land to urban and suburban sprawl have all had a negative impact on global food production (Pimentel et al. 1995; Brown and Kane 1994). Coupling these trends with continued population growth leads to concerns about future availability of food.

From 1950 to 1984, world grain production increased annually by 2.3 percent; from 1984 to 1993 it increased annually by only 1 percent. What's the worry? Crop yield is still increasing. But so are the human consumers of those crops, and the rate of population growth exceeds the growth rate of crop yields (Brown and Kane 1994).[6] The same trend has been predicted for global fisheries. World fish harvest peaked at 19 kg/person in 1989 and has been declining ever since. If the record catch rate from 1989 was maintained over the next several decades (an optimistic assumption), while the human population continued to grow at rates predicted by the United Nations, the per capita catch would be only 11 kg/person in 2030 (Brown 1994).

Human consumption of protein and grain varies considerably depending on geographical location. The average citizen of this planet consumes 323 kg of grain each year, whereas the average American citizen consumes 860 kg (Brown and Kane 1994). Americans consume so much grain because we feed it to cows, pigs, chickens, and other domestic animals. To feed the rest of the world as much grain as we are fed, global grain harvest would have to increase 2.6 times. Alternatively, the human population would have to decline to 40 percent of its current level. At the current rates of change of grain production and population growth, neither alternative seems likely.

This calculation leads us into the world of ethics. Is it morally right for some persons to consume in excess while others have so little? That is a moral question that has been with us for millennia, and I will not discuss it here. However, our current planetary situation provides us with a second moral dilemma that has become obvious in the past decade: Increasing levels of human activity are threatening the survival of other species on this planet.

My discussion of this problem begins with a couple of assertions: There is a limit to the number of people this planet can support. This limit is called the global carrying capacity. Determining that limit requires both scientific and moral judgment.

Ecologists have been studying carrying capacities for decades, and we know that the carrying capacity of a species is determined by the availability of resources and by the amount of resources required by each individual of a species, be that a human or a bacterium. The calculation of human carrying capacity thus requires a determination of the amount of resources required by a person, which is determined by the quality of life that is desired and the technology that is available to make resources available to humans (for example, Daily and Ehrlich 1992). There continue to be improvements in technology that permit more efficient utilization of resources and an improved quality of life with reduced use of resources. For example, a refrigerator manufactured in the early 1970s used over 1,700 kilowatt hours per year, whereas one manufactured in the mid-1990s uses one-third of that amount (Arms 1994). Although these improvements in technology will continue, ultimately there will be a limit to human numbers set by the physical limitations of our planet.

One can calculate an absolute physical limit to the number of people the planet can support based on its capacity to dissipate heat. When a physicist named Fremlin did this, he calculated that humans would reach that limit at 60 million billion people (Fremlin 1964, cited in Pulliam and Haddad 1994). That population size translates to 120 persons/m^2 of planetary surface (including oceans). Fremlin speculates on life at this time: Species not essential to human survival will be eliminated long before the population reaches this upper limit. Food will consist of directly synthesized fats, carbohydrates, and amino acids (I envision something like catfish pellets for humans). There will be "construction of 2000 story buildings over land and sea alike. . . . That would give 7.5 m^2 of floor space (a room about 9 feet on a side) for each person. Occasional . . , travel over a few hundred meters would be permissible . . . so that each individual could choose friends out of some ten million people, giving adequate social variety. . . . One could expect some ten million Shakespeares . . . to be alive at any one time." Is this the planet we want to call home?

The point of this exercise is that there is a limit to the number of people our planet can support. Deciding what that limit will be is an ethical decision that requires a collective vision of what kind of world we wish to inhabit. Humans are sentient beings with an aesthetic sense that enables us to see beauty in the wildness of nature and the diversity of life forms. For many of us, that beauty is what gives meaning to our lives. Yet there is no place on our planet untouched by the human hand. In some places, the touch is light—an altered atmosphere; elsewhere, humans dominate. We are a global presence.

A discussion of global carrying capacity requires a vision for the kind of world we want as well as an assessment of the resources available. Since I am an ecologist, I will start with an ecological assessment of resources. The amount of new plant tissue produced each year by green plants is called net primary productivity; this is what forms the base of the food web for humans and other species. Humans currently appropriate more than 40 percent of all terrestrial primary productivity, thereby reducing the resources available to other species (Vitousek et al. 1986). This appropriation includes both direct consumption as well as resources degraded by human activity and reduction in rates of primary productivity in response to anthropogenic stresses on plants. With current rates of resource consumption and human population growth, we could appropriate 80 percent of terrestrial primary productivity in sixty years, leaving only 20 percent for the millions of other species with whom we share this planet. This is not the world that my children want to inhabit.

We see one consequence of our appropriation of land, water, and air resources in the reduction of biological diversity. This is particularly apparent in threats to survival of aquatic species. More than 50 percent of all crayfish and mussel species, more than 30 percent of freshwater fish species, and 30 percent of amphibian species in the United States are rare (fewer than 10,000 individuals or 100 locales) or imperiled (fewer than 1,000 individuals) (Stolzenburg 1995). Aquatic species have been particularly damaged by our consumption and degradation of fresh water. The situation is no better in Europe, where 20–60 percent of the bird, mammal, and fish species are threatened (OECD 1991). The loss of species is not just in tropical rain forests; it is here in our own states and countries. We are threatening the continued existence of other species by the way we as humans lead our lives.

Applying the ecological concept of carrying capacity to humans has been criticized because it does not take into account human capacity for technological innovations that will increase carrying capacity and does not recognize the role of social, political, and economic institutions in determining a nation's carrying capacity (for example, Aiken 1980). Increased economic activity and enhanced trade can certainly increase a nation's carrying capacity, although that increase comes at the expense of other resources. Yet even if social, political, and economic systems were such that global resources were equitably distributed (something never achieved in all of human history), global resources are inadequate to support unlimited population growth. It is obvious that the agriculture of today can support a larger human population than could fifteenth-century agriculture. Human technological innovation in agriculture has increased the carrying capacity of the planet. Yet the planetary capacity to support continued innovation is not infinite, and the rate of innovation will not necessarily keep pace with human population growth rate. Humans also may not be willing to accept technological innovations that would increase global carrying capacity but that would require them to change long-established practices or behaviors rooted in religious beliefs or cultural history. In addition, multiple demands on limited resources are likely to limit technological progress, and new technologies often bring unintended consequences that alter essential resources. Even if unlimited growth of humans were technologically possible, it would be morally reprehensible because unlimited growth of humans would reduce the resources available to other species.

Not only are we a part of and dependent on the web of life on the planet but we also have a moral obligation to maintain that web. How much of the earth's resources should one species, Homo sapiens, appropriate for its use? We currently appropriate 40 percent of terrestrial net primary productivity. Is that amount morally defensible? The global dilemma translates into an individual moral decision: How large a proportion of earth's resources should a morally responsible human consume? Let us get personal: How large a proportion of earth's resources should I consume? This is one of the most important ethical questions confronting each of us. We answer it each day as we lead our lives. We must answer with care and be aware of the consequences of our answer. Your grandchildren and mine are counting on us.

NOTES

1. For example, *Bromus tectorum* is a weed that has invaded the western United States, and its growth rate is more responsive to increased CO_2 than is the growth rate of the native grasses with which it is competing (Smith, Strain, and Sharkey 1987).
2. For example, in the lower Mississippi River, concentrations of nitrate in river water have increased threefold since 1950 (Turner and Robelais 1991).
3. For example, deaths of children under five years of age decreased from over 200/1,000 in Ethiopia to less than 5/1,000 in Sweden, as the proportion of the population with access to safe drinking water increased from 19 percent to 99 percent (Engelman and LeRoy 1993).
4. Lead used in gasoline decreased from 50,000 tons per quarter in 1977 to 20,000 tons in 1980; during the same period, levels of lead in human blood decreased from 16 µg/dl to 6 µg/dl (Meybeck, Chapman, and Helmer 1989).
5. Per capita water availability in North America is over 17,000 m^3 (Raven, Berg, and Johnson 1995).
6. Per capita grain production has declined from 346 kg/person in 1984 to about 300 kg/person in 1993 (Brown 1994).

REFERENCES

Aiken, W. 1980. The "carrying capacity" equivocation. *Social Theory and Practice* 6:1–12.

Arms, K. 1994. *Environmental science.* New York: Saunders.

Barnola, J. M., D. Raynaud, Y. S. Korotkevitch, and C. Lorius. 1987. Vostok ice core: A 160,000-year record of atmospheric CO_2. *Nature* 329:408–14.

Bazzaz, F. A. 1990. The response of natural ecosystems to the rising global CO_2 levels. *Annual Review of Ecology and Systematics* 21:167–96.

Bazzaz, F. A., S. L. Miao, and P. M. Wayne. 1994. CO_2-induced enhancements of co-occurring tree species decline at different rates. *Oecologica* 96:478–82.

Brown, L. R. 1994. Facing food insecurity. In *State of the world 1994,* ed. Worldwatch Institute. New York: W. W. Norton, 177–97.

Brown, L. R., and H. Kane. 1994. *Full house.* New York: W. W. Norton.

Daily, G. C., and P. R. Ehrlich. 1992. Population, sustainability, and earth's carrying capacity. *BioScience* 42:761–71.

Engelman, R., and P. LeRoy. 1993. *Sustaining water: Population and the future of renewable water supplies*. Washington, D.C.: Population Action International.

Fajer, E. D., M. D. Bowers, and F. A. Bazzaz. 1989. The effects of increased carbon dioxide atmospheres on plant-insect herbivore interactions. *Science* 243: 1198–1200.

Fremlin, J. H. 1964. How many people can the world support? *New Scientist* 415:285–87.

Meybeck, M., D. V. Chapman, and R. Helmer. 1989. *Global freshwater quality*. United Nations Environment Program. Cambridge, Mass.: Blackwell.

Meyer, J. L. 1994. The dance of nature: New concepts in ecology. *Chicago Kent Law Review* 69:875–86.

Norby, R. J., J. Pastor, and J. M. Melillo. 1986. Carbon-nitrogen interactions in CO_2-enriched white oak: Physiological and long-term perspectives. *Tree Physiology* 2:233–41.

OECD. 1991. *State of the environment*. Paris: Organization for Economic Cooperation and Development.

Pimentel, D., C. Harvey, P. Resosudarmo, K. Sinclair, D. Kurz, M. McNair, S. Crist, L. Shpritz, L. Fitton, R. Saffouri, and R. Blair. 1995. Environmental and economic costs of soil erosion and conservation benefits. *Science* 267: 1117–23.

Postel, S. 1992. *The last oasis*. New York: W. W. Norton.

Pulliam, H. R., and N. M. Haddad. 1994. Human population growth and the carrying capacity concept. *Bulletin of the Ecological Society of America* 75: 141–56.

Raven, P. H., L. R. Berg, and G. B. Johnson. 1995. *Environment*. New York: Saunders.

Schultze, E. D. 1989. Air pollution and forest decline in a spruce (*Picea abies*) forest. *Science* 244:776–83.

Smith, S. D., B. R. Strain, and T. D. Sharkey. 1987. Effects of CO_2 enrichment on four Great Basin grasses. *Functional Ecology* 1:139–43.

Stolzenburg, W. 1995. Scorecard of scarcity. *Nature Conservancy Magazine*, May–June 1995, 6.

Turner, R. E., and N. N. Robelais. 1991. Changes in Mississippi River water quality this century. *BioScience* 41:140–47.

Vitousek, P. M. 1994. Beyond global warming: Ecology and global change. *Ecology* 75:1861–76.

Vitousek, P. M., P. R. Ehrlich, A. H. Ehrlich, and P. A. Matson. 1986. Human appropriation of the products of photosynthesis. *BioScience* 36:368–73.

EUGENE HARGROVE

Taking Environmental Ethics Seriously

The Challenge before Us

Environmental ethics research began hesitantly in the 1970s as philosophers made tentative efforts toward the creation of a field within professional philosophy. It gained speed at the end of the decade with the founding of the journal *Environmental Ethics*, which provided a forum for debate and gave environmental ethicists reasonable publication opportunities. Until then, environmental ethics papers were published on a token basis by mainstream philosophy periodicals, usually one or two papers per year at most. With the publication of a number of single-authored theories in the late 1980s, environmental ethicists became major players within applied ethics and philosophy. Environmental ethics, however, is still not having much impact in philosophy doctoral programs. Although there are at least fifteen environmental history doctoral programs in the United States, graduate education in environmental ethics is primarily the province of M.A. programs in philosophy. The applied doctoral program at Bowling Green State University, which has a strong environmental ethics component, is perhaps the one exception, but it started as an applied M.A. program, not as a traditional program. To date, no traditional doctoral program in philosophy in the United States has a strong focus on environmental philosophy. Most of the major fig-

ures in environmental ethics, including Holmes Rolston III, J. Baird Calli-
cott, Jim Cheney, Karen Warren, and Max Oelschlaeger, teach in philosophy programs offering the B.A. or the M.A. but not the Ph.D. and sometimes no degree program at all.

Although this neglect at major institutions offering traditional philosophy programs may be rapidly changing, with some tenured professors beginning to take an interest, environmental ethics remains an esoteric field
as far as environmental affairs is concerned, and it still has little or no influence on what environmental professionals do on a daily basis. Environmental ethicists have not succeeded in developing the kind of relationship, for example, that medical ethicists have with doctors, lawyers, and
policymakers. The medical community wants something very different
from medical ethics than environmental professionals want from environmental ethics. Medical ethicists are generally asked to participate in the
resolution of tough decisions which members of the medical community do not want to resolve themselves. For example, philosophers rather
than doctors were called upon to define the moment of death for organ-
transplant policy. Death was considered to be a philosophical rather than
a factual matter because medical procedures involving transplants require
a "dead" person with live organs. Essentially, matters of this kind are a
pre-law exercise, which permits the medical community to defend itself
on the grounds that it consulted experts.

Environmental professionals have little interest in having philosophers
make tough decisions for them. I know of only one group: the conservation biologists who oversee the species survival plans for endangered
species at zoological parks. Tough cases are generated in this area of environmental affairs because there are conflicts between environmental
intuitions (the province of environmental ethics) and animal welfare intuitions (the province of animal rights and animal liberation). Actions involved in carrying out these plans generated obvious conflicts between the
two sets of intuitions because the concerns of animal welfare ethics for the
individual are not entirely compatible with the holistic concerns of environmental ethics for species. Because crossover conflicts of this kind are
rare in environmental affairs, there is little call for help in resolving tough
cases analogous to those handled by medical ethicists.

The interest of environmental professionals is not in tough cases but in
justification. Although there is frequently little disagreement among en-

vironmental professionals about what should be done in specific cases, there is a general feeling that most of the ethical reasons that can be given for these decisions are weak. A very good example of the basic problem can be found in *Among the Elephants* by Ian Douglas-Hamilton, who was then a graduate student doing research in Africa for his Ph.D. dissertation at Oxford University. He was studying the relationship of African elephants to acacia trees in a national park in Tanzania called Manyara. The elephants were demolishing most of the trees. Douglas-Hamilton's job was to figure out what to do: cull the elephants or let the botanical carnage continue. About this matter, he writes:

> Here was an issue that could only be decided in relation to aesthetic, economic or political considerations. In ecological terms the Seronera tree damage was insignificant. The very desire to preserve the animals was a subjective statement of faith in the animal's intrinsic worth. It was a feeling possessed by most of the scientists there, who regarded the wildebeest migration with the same awe that others feel for the *Mona Lisa,* but they would not admit this sentiment into their arguments because it could not be backed up by facts; the right and wrong of aesthetics being imponderables not open to scientific analysis.[1]

The problem was that no one connected with the park wanted to shoot the elephants. They wanted to protect the elephants, moreover, because they admired the animals and felt that they had great aesthetic value and intrinsic worth. Nevertheless, they did not believe that these feelings could be part of a professional justification for not shooting the elephants. Given that such justifications were closed off for him, Douglas-Hamilton concluded that he was supposed to find some facts that would independently justify this position so that the aesthetic considerations would not have to be mentioned.

The result was what George Orwell called "doublethink," which he defined in his novel *1984* as "the power of holding two contradictory beliefs in one's mind simultaneously, and accepting both of them."[2] In this case, Douglas-Hamilton felt that he was supposed to use certain kinds of values that are generally held about elephants to determine his conclusions, but at the same time to pretend that these values were not involved in the determination of the solution, which was supposed to be based instead on an ecological, scientific proof. This type of sleight of hand, which is widely practiced in environmental affairs, can cause severe feelings of guilt among those not able to handle the deception (including self-deception). The most serious problem, however, is that the practice prevents any real policy debate, since the justification officially given has nothing to do with the actual reasons that determined the decision or policy.

I encountered this problem when I was invited as a humanities consultant to participate in a capstone seminar for environmental managers at a Big Ten school. I soon realized that the students had been inoculated against values of virtually any kind. Every time graduate students made presentations, they began with protestations that when they became environmental professionals, they would always provide objective information that was entirely value-free and that they would never reveal their "biases," which they considered to be the equivalent of any subjective judgments that they might make. Disturbed by these automatic disputations, I pointed out that *subjective* did not mean "biased." Rather, it simply meant that a person had a mind and made judgments. These judgments, moreover, were not biased if they could be justified in ways that would win extensive if not universal agreement. Throughout the sessions, nevertheless, they continued to hold that any position that was not objective in the sense of being value-free was subjective, biased, arbitrary, emotional, and therefore unprofessional.

When I tried to explain that some objectivity could be achieved by appealing to our common cultural heritage and values, the teacher insisted that we had no common values, that each person individually and independently invented his or her own values, and that the values of one person had no relationship to the values of anyone else, making common agreement impossible. Neither the teacher nor her students, however, had any difficulty reaching agreement about economic values because they considered these values to be facts. They were acceptable because they were quantified preferences in terms of willingness to pay, gleaned from surveys in which representative groups of people were asked how much they were willing to spend to keep, for example, an endangered species in existence. Through such surveys, environmental professionals can determine with great precision that while $2.37 per household is an acceptable amount to justify protecting an endangered species, the addition of another penny might be so excessive that it would be best to just let the unfortunate species go, on the grounds that protecting it is just too expensive.

Although the results of these surveys appear to produce "factual" values, free of subjectivity and bias, there are many problems with this approach.[3] The chief problem is that many respondents find the entire exercise inappropriate, since they consider species to be priceless—that is, off the economic scale—and they refuse to commit themselves to $2.37, $2.38, or any other amount. Like Douglas-Hamilton, they consider species to be valuable in the same sense that such works of art as the *Mona Lisa* can be said to be valuable and they enter qualitative protest bids that cannot be quantified, added up, and averaged. Because such protest bids frequently make up 20–50 percent of the survey results, quantification can only be accomplished by throwing out the qualitative results. The justification for their omission, from the economists' standpoint, however, is that the participants have willingly chosen to let their preferences remain "unknown and unaccounted for."[4] As Rolston notes, savvy respondents may decide, instead of making protest bids, to choose the largest amount of money they feel the economists might be willing to accept.[5] Given that some respondents play the game as the economists wish, some weight their responses upward, risking exclusion from the data pool, and some declare the species to be priceless, guaranteeing exclusion, the results of this strange mix can hardly be declared to be simply a matter of facts.

The peculiar status of economics as a "factual" science is probably the major obstacle to environmental policy and decision making based on environmental ethics. This obstruction was historically intentional. In 1970, for example, Allen Kneese testified before a congressional committee that environmental economics eliminated the need for the development of an environmental ethic.[6] Although economics is usually presented as a factual matter, thereby eliminating, as Kneese claims, the need for philosophy and ethics, it is actually a naive blending of three fairly recent philosophical positions: utilitarianism from the middle of the nineteenth century, pragmatism from the turn of the century, and logical positivism from the early twentieth century. Each contributes to the elimination of value from consideration in policy and decision making.

Utilitarianism in its original form defined good as pleasure. One was supposed to make calculations about the total amount of pleasure that people would experience in order to determine the greatest good for the greatest number. The problem with this approach (which Aristotle brought up more than two thousand years ago and which has been ignored ever since utilitarianism took hold at the policy level) is that one cannot define good as pleasure because it is obvious that people frequently take pleasure in bad things. If pleasure becomes the standard for what is good, then anything anybody takes pleasure in becomes good, and *good* becomes a relative term that is completely meaningless.

Pragmatism in its original form defined good in terms of use. Like utilitarianism, it proposes a simplification of value. Major efforts were made by some pragmatists, particularly John Dewey, to eliminate intrinsic value in favor of instrumental value. This concept of value, which was fully compatible with Gifford Pinchot's conservation and resource management approach, has contributed to the problem initially created by the utilitarians. When the utilitarian's concept of good as pleasure was combined with the pragmatist's concept of good as use, environmental managers came to conceive of the natural beauty as the instrumental triggering of feelings of pleasure in park visitors.

This view of aesthetic value frequently presents environmental professionals with unsolvable dilemmas today. In order to increase the value of the natural object that they are protecting and displaying, managers try to increase visitation. More visitors means more instrumental triggerings of pleasure, which means the generation of more value. In most cases, however, the increased traffic begins to damage the park, threatening the end of the value-generation process. Because the value of the natural object is seen as instrumental, and the idea that the object has intrinsic value, that is, is valuable for its own sake and not simply as a pleasure generator, is not taken into consideration, managers are not able to eliminate visitation in order to protect the object from further damage. This is the standard approach in art museums, where art objects are routinely viewed as being valuable for their own sake. Saddled with the truncated instrumental value approach, the managers are limited in their policy options simply to considering alternatives that will generate the most instrumental value for the most people over the longest time. Eliminating visitation, which brings instrumental-value generation to zero and strips the object of value, is equivalent to the value loss that would occur with the immediate destruction of the object, both of which are unacceptable alternatives. Thus, the managers have to commit themselves to a policy that will prolong instrumental-value generation as long as possible. In this way, the aesthetic consumption of the object becomes the only practical option. All of the alternatives involve the eventual destruction of the object. The policymakers simply determine the length of time that the object will continue to exist.

Although the pragmatists thought they had successfully reduced all value to use value and eliminated intrinsic value entirely, the people who were supposed to use the new system were not entirely convinced. The result has been confusion, not clarity. Once environmental professionals were fully trained to think exclusively in instrumental terms and were no longer able to think in any other way (at least officially), they began to feel that something was missing. Intuitively recognizing that there ought to be some things in nature that are valuable for their own sake, they began complaining that "nature ought to have rights." Robbed of the appropriate terminology (intrinsic value), they turned to an inappropriate one—political and moral rights for nature. Today environmental professionals know that their value system is inadequate, but they have not been left with enough value terminology to articulate the problem without metaphorical reference to rights for nature.

When philosophers first began research into environmental ethics, they noted that environmentalists were talking about rights for nature. Although almost a decade of debate followed, environmental ethicists failed to come up with a theory that could support rights for nature. The reason that these efforts failed is that rights are associated with the interests of individuals. The things that environmentalists want to protect in nature—ecosystems and species—are neither individuals nor things that in any clear, determinate sense have interests. To have a viable rights theory, the interests that the rights are supposed to protect have to be the interests of all of the living things in an ecosystem or the interests of the members of each species. The sum of these interests, in either case, does not equal the interests of the ecosystem or each species in the ecosystem. For example, in the case of species, the deaths of some individuals, the unfit, are supposed to benefit the species. Likewise, the healthy functioning of an ecosystem requires the death of innumerable plants and animals on a daily basis.

Environmental professionals do begin acting in a way that is compatible with species rights when a species becomes endangered. When the number of individuals in an endangered species becomes so low that we know how many are left, efforts to protect the species become so intensive that it is almost as if the interests of each individual were being protected, suggesting that a rights approach might be plausible after all. However, the object of the preservation effort is to bring the population back to a level at which no one will care what happens to any particular individual member of the species, as long as it suffers its personal calamity in a natural manner. Rights are absolute. They do not increase and disappear as the members of a particular group wax and wane. Of course, rights comparable to human rights could be given to the individual members of wild species or ecosystems. However, properly acting on such rights would mean the elimination of wild nature as we protected it not only from ourselves but also from itself.

According to logical positivism, the last of the three positions upon which modern economics is based, only those statements which are scientifically verifiable have meaning. Armed with this dogma, the logical positivists launched an attack on ethics, aesthetics, and religion, claiming that ethical, aesthetic, and religious statements are unverifiable and therefore meaningless: when someone makes an ethical statement or asserts an ethical value, all that he or she is doing is expressing an arbitrary, subjective emotion. It is this philosophical theory, the emotivist theory of value, that is the basis for the claims of the graduate students at the Big Ten school that any reference to values would simply be an expression of a personal bias, an expression of personal feeling irrelevant to any matter of fact.

The importance of logical positivism for economic theory is clear from the opening pages of Milton Friedman's *Essays in Positive Economics.* Economics was able to declare itself to be a science—thereby becoming "factual"—by adopting the logical positivist's approach to fact and value. In the first two paragraphs of his book, Friedman points out—on the authority of John Maynard Keynes, who wrote *The Scope and Method of Political Economy* in 1887—that one can distinguish between *is* and *ought* and that the economist doesn't need to think about *ought.*

In principle, positive economics is independent of any particular ethical position or normative judgments. As Keynes says, it deals with "what is," not with "what ought to be." Its task is to provide a system of generalizations that can be used to make correct predictions about the consequences of any change in circumstances. Its performance is to be judged by the precision, scope, and conformity with experience of the predictions it yields. In short, positive economics is, or can be, an "objective" science, in precisely the same sense as any of the physical sciences.[7]

By eliminating the *ought,* economists are able to become neutral with regard to the results of their surveys of preference statements. They simply record the preferences, throw out the protest bids, and add up or quantify the remaining preferences. Although the preference statements remain value or *ought* statements, the statements about the *number* of preferences of various kinds resulting from the survey are factual or *is* statements. By focusing on these factual statements and making no judgments about the preferences of the respondents (thereby remaining neutral), economics achieves its factual status. The result is said to be value-free or factual statements about values.

This positivistic position on *is* and *ought,* though little noted, has had an enormous impact on environmental affairs. It is not, however, a reasoned or argued position. When Friedman presents it in his book, for example, he simply cites as authority the opinion of a minor political economist of the late nineteenth century. Usually, when the view is taught, no defense is provided at all. It is presented as a fact, the way the world is, not as a recent philosophical position that has largely been abandoned in contemporary philosophy. Because it is a philosophical dogma which has been uncritically accepted as the way that scientists and social scientists are supposed to think, it is difficult to dispute. When environmental ethicists tell environmental professionals that they should—indeed, must—take into account values as well as facts, they are usually greeted by yawns and requests to move on to more important matters. They are unwilling to listen because they have been successfully inoculated against thinking in value terms. Both the teacher and the students at the seminar I attended were amazed that I even brought the subject up. For them, the matter was beyond dispute, beyond discussion. It was part of the unquestioned framework within which they viewed the world.

The reaction of environmental professionals is even worse when *intrinsic value* is mentioned, because of the distaste for that term as it has trickled down out of pragmatism. Normally environmental professionals are willing to go to great lengths to avoid using the term, which they think is quaint and old-fashioned. In 1993 I participated in a conference in the

Yukon, at which I was supposed to speak about the relationship of a draft wolf management policy and the Yukon Environment Act.[8] Being a philosopher, I was interested in finding out what the drafters of the policy had to say about intrinsic value. It was difficult to find, however, because the management policy was written overtly in instrumental and economic terms. Nevertheless, the intrinsic value of the wolves was discussed in one short section. Although the term was mentioned once in the first paragraph along with a reference to *inherent value,* the section was entitled "The Non-consumptive Use of Wolves."[9] I noted that while *non-consumptive use* captured some of what *intrinsic value* was supposed to mean, to completely cover the full range of meaning without using the actual term the section needed to be retitled "The Non-economic, Non-consumptive, Non-instrumental Non-use of Wolves." This title would have more accurately captured the spirit of the section which dealt with the intrinsic value of wolves by describing it negatively in terms of what it is not: non-consumptive, non-instrumental, and non-economic use.

The development of these "non-terms" parallels a fictional language project called "Newspeak" in George Orwell's *1984.* The Newspeak project was an attempt to redefine and eliminate words so that it would eventually be impossible to express a wide variety of ethical and political ideas. A philologist working on the project explains the project in this way:

> We're getting the language into final shape. . . . You think, I dare say, that our chief job is inventing new words. But not a bit! We're destroying words—scores of them, hundreds of them every day. We're cutting the language down to the bone. . . . It's a beautiful thing, the destruction of words. Of course the great wastage is in the verbs and the adjectives, but there are hundreds of nouns that have to be gotten rid of as well. It isn't only synonyms. After all, what justification is there for a word which is simply the opposite of some other word? A word contains its opposite in its self. Take "good," for instance. If you have a word like "good," what need is there for a word like "bad"? "Ungood" will do just as well—better, because it's an exact opposite, which the other is not. Or again, if you want a stronger version of "good," what sense is there in having a whole string of vague useless words like "excellent" and "splendid" and all the rest of them? "Plusgood" covers the meaning, or "doubleplusgood" if you want

something stronger still. Of course we use those forms already, but in the final version of Newspeak there'll be nothing else. In the end the whole notion of goodness and badness will be covered by only six words—in reality, only one.[10]

While it is not very likely that economists read *1984* and intentionally tried to carry out an environmental Newspeak project of their own, their economic nonjargon is having the same effect in environmental affairs, for this nontalk is making it increasingly difficult to think except in economic terms. For example, the terms *aesthetic value* and *natural beauty* refer to a three- to four-century tradition which has developed out of landscape painting, nature poetry and prose, landscape gardening, and the natural history sciences. Although *natural beauty* can be precisely and exhaustively defined in terms of that tradition, environmental professionals have been trained that the term has no meaning of any kind—that natural beauty is arbitrarily in the eye of the beholder and not imbedded in evolving social ideals. When they have to deal with natural beauty, they are therefore expected to translate the aesthetic value of nature into travel costs: for example, the cost of gasoline, air or rail travel, film, souvenirs, lodging, and meals. Although this definition of aesthetic value has nothing to do with the actual definition of aesthetic value (which is grounded in the aesthetic traditions of the modern period), it is used by environmental professionals because it produces dollar values that can be declared objective and value-free. The danger of this procedure is that it may eventually lead to the replacement of the actual definition of *aesthetic value* with an economic one that has nothing to do with aesthetics at all. If this redefinition is successful, there may eventually come a time when it is no longer possible to think in aesthetic terms, and references to the beauty of nature will be reduced to the cost of going on vacation. When this conversion is complete, aesthetic value will become a weak economic value. This conversion will parallel changes in the meaning of the word *use*. The title of the section on the intrinsic value of wolves was "The Non-consumptive Use of Wolves," not "The Non-consumptive Non-use of Wolves," showing that instrumental value is now so dominant in environmental policy that it is linguistically no longer possible to value anything except as a use. When *aesthetic value* is completely converted, the original meaning of the term, like *use,* will gradually become unintelligible.

This translation project has important implications in environmental law. Most environmental laws include lists of values that are supposed to be promoted, and economic value is usually intentionally left out of these laws. The Wilderness Act of 1964, for example, is supposed to ensure "that an increasing population, accompanied by expanding settlement and growing mechanization, does not occupy and modify all areas within the United States," and it includes a number of values: ecological, geological, scientific, educational, scenic, and historical. The National Environmental Policy Act of 1970, which is supposed to curb, in particular, "the profound influences of population growth, high-density urbanization, industrial expansion, resource exploitation and new and expanding technological advances," refers not only to instrumental values that are safe, helpful, and productive, but also to values that are aesthetically and intrinsically pleasing, including historical, cultural, and nature value and diversity and variety values. The Endangered Species Act of 1973, which is supposed to impede "economic growth and development untempered by adequate concern and conservation," is supposed to promote a whole series of values. Specifically, the law states that endangered "species of fish, wildlife, and plants are of esthetic, ecological, educational, historical, recreational, and scientific value to the Nation and its people."[11]

Because the Endangered Species Act, in particular, explicitly cites "economic growth and development" as the cause of the problem and omits economic value from the list of values to be considered, it is certainly at a minimum contrary to the spirit of the law, and it is most likely illegal, to translate the values listed in the law into economic values. When these values are translated into economic values, they become *weak* economic values that cannot hold their own in cost-benefit analysis, since the economic benefits of the destruction of any particular wild species usually outweigh, for example, the aesthetic value defined in terms of the cost of buying gasoline, sleeping in motels, and eating at restaurants or triggering momentary feelings of pleasure. For aesthetic value to win, the policymakers must give additional weight of some kind to the aesthetic value beyond what the weak economic definition permits. In such cases, travel costs have to be supplemented by aesthetic value in the traditional sense, while simultaneously denying that the traditional value is being used.

It could be said that I slight a good many cases where scientists have come looking for philosophers. For example, the Society for Conservation Biology reserves a position on its board of governors for ethics and philosophy. Likewise, the American Zoo and Aquarium Association has been very involved with philosophers with regard to species survival plans. The Office of Technology Assessment almost invariably put philosophers on its task forces. The Society of American Foresters when reconsidering its land ethic published an article coauthored by a philosopher in its *Journal of Forestry*. Other journals, such as *Conservation Biology, Bioscience,* and *Sierra,* have published articles on environmental ethics. It could even be argued that the existence of the value language in environmental laws is tacit counterevidence to my grim evaluation of the role of environmental ethics in environmental affairs. Note, however, that the U.S. government has not been very supportive of funding for environmental ethics–related research, since the field came into existence after those laws were enacted. Although the National Science Foundation has steadily funded environmental ethics projects, from 1982 until 1995 the National Endowment for the Humanities officially refused to provide funding for applied philosophy. It was the official policy not to fund research grants that used the words *environment* or *value*. At the beginning of the Reagan administration, for instance, the name of the Science, Technology, and Human Values Program was changed to the Science and Technology Program, and researchers, before being funded, were required to demonstrate that their results would be of historical but not contemporary value. Although the NEH is no longer ideologically committed to suppressing applied research, massive budget cuts have prevented it from continuing tentative efforts to make amends. The Office of Technology Assessment, of course, no longer exists. With regard to environmental publications, some (for example, *Sierra*) have reduced their commitment to publishing environmental ethics when surveys showed that many readers were not interested or found the articles too difficult to read. More generally, the news media seldom make any effort to use environmental philosophers as sources. Unlike medical ethicists, environmental ethicists are not regarded as resources for news stories. Despite having worked with environmental philosophers in the past, the Society of Environmental Journalists and the international Federation of Environmental Journalists refuse to include information about environmental ethics on their website.

Mark Sagoff has noted that we are both citizens and consumers—that we have both citizen preferences and consumer preferences.[12] Consumer preferences are simply a matter of how we feel. They do not need to be justified. An introspective check of how one feels is all the justification required. Citizen preferences, however, are not feelings but, rather, opinions and beliefs. They cannot be justified simply by reflecting on how we feel. Rather, their justification requires reasons and arguments. They can be debated. On the basis of this debate, we can conclude that some preferences are right and that others are wrong. Although the views of the individual are important, they achieve their significance in terms of our traditions, our ideals, in terms of what we stand for as a nation. The values that are listed in such laws as the Endangered Species Act are not the feelings that economists survey as consumer preferences but, rather, the ideals that have evolved over centuries and represent not how we *feel* as individuals but what we *are* as a society.

In the Middle Ages, educated people were taught that nature was not beautiful. Nevertheless, in the early modern period Europeans learned to appreciate nature aesthetically, and this appreciation became the basis for the environmental movement as it exists today.[13] In this century, in the late modern or postmodern period, people are being taught that values in general are irrelevant and that environmental policy can be formulated in a value-free manner, despite the fact that this training is counterintuitive. In the sciences and the social sciences, it continues to inhibit the development of an environmental ethic. I have referred to it as a kind of inoculation against value training. If this inoculation proves to be successful in convincing policymakers that they can continue to operate in a value-free manner, removing even wistful claims that "nature ought to have rights," there will probably be no future for environmental ethics or the environmental movement. It is this intellectual—or perhaps anti-intellectual—issue which will determine whether the postmodern period will be an age of ecology or an age of economics. Such is the challenge before us.

NOTES

1. Ian and Oria Douglas-Hamilton, *Among the Elephants* (New York: Viking Press, 1975), 77.

2. George Orwell, *Orwell's* Nineteen Eighty-Four: *Text, Sources, Criticism*, ed. Irving Howe (New York: Harcourt, Brace and World, 1963), 95.

3. See, for example, Holmes Rolston III, "Valuing Wildlands," *Environmental Ethics* 7 (1985): 34–35.

4. Herman Leonard and Richard Zeckhauser, "Cost-Benefit Analysis Applied to Risks: Its Philosophy and Legitimacy," in *Values at Risk,* ed. Douglas MacLean (Totowa, N.J.: Rowman and Littlefield, 1986), 3. See Mark Sagoff's discussion of this matter in *The Economy of the Earth: Philosophy, Law, and the Environment* (Cambridge: Cambridge University Press, 1988), 88.

5. Rolston, "Valuing Wildlands," 34.

6. Prepared statement of Dr. Allen V. Kneese, *The Environmental Decade: Hearings before a Subcommittee of the Committee on Government Operations,* House, 91st Cong., 2d sess., 1970, 191. See Sagoff's discussion of Kneese's views in *The Economy of the Earth,* 3–7.

7. Milton Friedman, *Essays in Positive Economics* (Chicago: University of Chicago Press, 1953), 4.

8. See Eugene C. Hargrove, "Science, Ethics, and the Care of Ecosystems," in *Northern Protected Areas and Wilderness,* ed. Juri Peepre and Bob Jickling (Whitehorse: Canadian Parks and Wilderness Society and Yukon College, 1995), 44–61.

9. Yukon Wolf Management Planning Team, *The Yukon Wolf Conservation and Management Plan,* 31 August 1992, sec. 5.0, p. 5.

10. Orwell, *Orwell's* Nineteen Eighty-Four, 23–24.

11. Public Law 88–577, *U.S. Statutes at Large* 78 (1964): 90–91; Public Law 91–190, *U.S. Statutes at Large* 83 (1970): 852; Public Law 93–205, *U.S. Statutes at Large* 87 (1973): 884.

12. Sagoff, *Economy of the Earth,* 7–8.

13. See Marjorie Hope Nicolson, *Mountain Gloom and Mountain Glory: The Development of the Aesthetic of the Infinite* (New York: Norton, 1963).

LIBRARY
BRYAN COLLEGE
DAYTON, TENN. 37321

MARK SAGOFF

Is the Economy Too Big
for the Environment?

Since the 1970s, many environmentalists have predicted imminent and intractable shortages of energy and other raw materials that support economic growth. The scale of the global economy, they argue, has
begun to exceed the carrying capacity of the earth. Paul Ehrlich (1974,
33), a leading advocate of this view, wrote in *The End of Affluence* that
"energy shortages will be with us for the rest of the century, and that before 1985 mankind will enter a genuine age of scarcity in which many
things besides energy will be in short supply." [1]
More recently, a group of scientists leading a new movement, "ecological economics," has reasserted the belief that the global economy has become unsustainable in relation to the world's resource base. A leading
ecological economist, Herman Daly, joined Ehrlich in predicting general
scarcities to occur in the "medium-run period of one generation or one
average lifetime, say, twenty-five to seventy-five years" (Daly 1991c).
Modeler Donella Meadows concurred that our "use of many essential
resources and generation of many kinds of pollutants have already sur-
passed rates that are physically sustainable." She predicts that without
"significant reductions in material and energy flows, there will be in the
coming decades an uncontrolled decline in per capita food output, energy use, and industrial production" (Meadows, Meadows, and Randers
1992, xv–xvi).

Is there a general relationship between the weight or size of the economy—the amount of goods and services we produce and consume—and the environmental problems that we face? The effects of DDT on pelicans, CFCs on stratospheric ozone, phosphate detergents on lakes, among many other disasters, show that specific pollutants damage particular aspects of the environment. Should we be concerned, however, only with a list of particular "spillovers" and "externalities"? Or do we think that these are symptomatic of a more general problem in the way that the size of the economy as a whole relates to constraints that the physical environment imposes? If so, should we join ecological economists in calling for a small economy for a small planet?

Two Strategies for Protecting the Environment

This essay will examine the controversy between two ways of answering these questions. The first proposes that specific pollutants, along with a few ill-advised policies and practices, generate most of our environmental woes. This strategy would address environmental problems on an ad hoc or case-by-case basis, primarily by regulating markets to ensure that the prices of goods and services reflect the full social costs—including the environmental costs—of producing them.

This first approach recommends, therefore, that we apply engineering and management "fixes" to deal with particular market or policy failures. This happened, for example, with respect to stratospheric ozone. When scientists reached a consensus that CFCs endanger the ozone layer, governments moved to reduce loadings, and corporations started to look for safer refrigerants and propellants. To be sure, particular challenges, such as the greenhouse effect, may call for large-scale conversions away from coal to other sources of energy. But even greenhouse gases pose a determinate challenge that calls for scientific study and then for an appropriate technical response (Schelling 1992).

Many mainstream economists adopt the first approach and thus reject the idea that the natural environment imposes immovable limits to economic expansion. In its 1992 *World Development Report,* for example, the World Bank attacks the view that "greater economic activity inevitably hurts the environment." The Bank says, "According to this view, as populations and incomes rise, a growing economy will require more inputs (thus depleting the earth's 'sources') and will produce more emissions and wastes (overburdening the earth's 'sinks.') As the scale of economic activity increases, the earth's 'carrying capacity' will be exceeded. In reality, of course, the relationships between inputs and outputs and the overall effects of economic activity on the environment are constantly changing" (38).

The second strategy, which is presented most forcefully in the new discipline of ecological economics, argues that as economic activity expands, it threatens the environment in general, systematic, modal, and endemic ways. Supporters of this second view contend that it is not particular pollutants or practices but economic activity as a whole or as we know it that strains overall ecological limits and threatens to exceed the "carrying capacity" of biospheric systems. "Economic growth, which is an increase in quantity, cannot be sustainable indefinitely on a finite planet" (Costanza, Daly, and Bartholomew 1991, 7).

This second approach asserts that the natural environment limits the "size" or "scale" of the economy in two ways. First, we have "entered a new era in which the limiting factor in development is no longer man-made capital but remaining natural capital." Natural capital, according to those who take this view, comprises natural resource flows, for example, "forests, fish populations and petroleum deposits." In an earlier era, one could acquire more of these resources by investing in man-made capital such as fishing boats and drilling rigs. Today, timber "is limited by remaining forests, not sawmill capacity; fish catch is limited by fish populations, not by fishing boats; crude oil is limited by remaining petroleum deposits, not by pumping and drilling capacity" (Costanza, Daly, and Bartholomew 1991, 8).

Second, the natural environment limits economic expansion because it cannot absorb vast amounts of wastes. As Herman Daly (1992, 190) puts this point: "The ecosystem is under no obligation to respond to increasing stress by sacrificing its services in the order of their increasing importance to us, conveniently giving economists a 'well-behaved' marginal cost function."[2]

Are mainstream economists correct in believing that the world economy can continue to grow as long as the appropriate market prices guide the way we use resources? Should we believe the "ecological" economists, in contrast, who say that remaining stocks of natural capital constitute the limiting factor in economic development or growth?

The Debate between Mainstream and Ecological Economics

Economics is always an instrumental science; it does not deliberate about ends but only about the means to an end, namely, the satisfaction of wants and desires, whatever they may be. It eschews moral arguments about what is intrinsically or objectively better or worse, right or wrong. It does not talk about the beauty of nature, for example, but about the "amenity" benefits for which individuals are willing to pay. Economics does not conjecture on the nature of the good life but leaves every person to be the judge of his or her own welfare.

The central difference between ecological and mainstream economics, insofar as they represent social sciences rather than moral philosophies, has to do with the benefit stream each believes that humanity may extract from the natural environment. Ecological economists, as we have seen, believe that "natural capital"—in which they include both sources of raw materials and sinks for wastes—sets limits on growth that the global economy has reached or even exceeded. Mainstream economists, in contrast, believe that intelligence or ingenuity frees us, as Barnett and Morse (1963, 11) have written, "to choose among an indefinitely large number of alternatives. There is no reason to believe that these alternatives will reduce to one that entails increasing cost—that it must sometime prove impossible to escape quantitative diminishing returns."

Ecological and mainstream economists, then, offer instrumental or prudential rather than moral, aesthetic, or religious reasons for protecting Nature. Mainstream economics, however, has always urged humanity to conquer, control, or manipulate nature whenever that would maximize the long-term benefits that human beings obtain. Ecological economists believe that the global economy cannot grow much further within the earth's ecological and resource constraints; therefore, they urge us to restrict or rein in economic activity.

Mainstream economists take the view that the limits to knowledge are the only limits to growth. They might point out that when two hundred

Pilgrims came to New England in 1620, half of them died in the first winter of cold, starvation, and disease. Today, perhaps 20 million Americans live in New England. Has the resource base grown by five orders of magnitude? No, what has changed, according to the mainstream position, is the knowledge base. Resources, indeed, are simply functions of knowledge or technology, in this view. As knowledge increases, so also resources increase, for we learn to make productive what is plentiful, for example, by turning sand into computer chips.

Ecological economists, in contrast, reject this appeal to knowledge and technology as a Faustian bargain. Herman Daly (1985, 274–75) rejects the idea that "technology and resource substitution [ingenuity] . . . can continuously outrun depletion and pollution." Growth faces limits. To "delude ourselves into believing that growth is still possible and desirable if only we label it 'sustainable' or color it 'green' will just delay the inevitable transition and make it more painful" (Daly 1993e, 268). We have "entered a new era in which the limiting factor in development is no longer man-made capital but remaining natural capital" (Costanza, Daly, and Bartholomew 1991, 8).[3] Other ecological economists agree: "Natural capital is rapidly becoming more and more scarce" (Folke et al. 1994, 9).

Mainstream economists question this view and tend instead to agree with management expert Peter Drucker that the limiting factor in economic growth is knowledge, not capital, whether natural or human-made. Where there is effective management, Drucker (1993, 45) writes, "that is, the application of knowledge to knowledge, we can always obtain the other resources." By this, Drucker means that human ingenuity enables the economy—to use Daly's phrasing—continually to outrun pollution and depletion. From this perspective, "greenhouse" gases, for example, present a management problem, perhaps to be solved by a CO_2 tax to improve "renewable" energy (such as solar) technologies. Likewise, the depletion of one raw material—whale oil for illumination and lubricants, for example—simply demands ingenuity to obtain the same benefits from some more plentiful resource.

The idea that knowledge is the key resource reflects theoretical results that Robert Solow presented in 1956 (Solow 1970, 77) to the effect that economic growth depends "simply on the rate of [labor augmenting] technological change."[4] Solow also found empirically that "most of the

growth of the economy over the last century had been due to technological progress" (Stiglitz 1990, 53).[5] Economists following Solow have
adopted a standard model of growth that contains essentially only two
factors: knowledge and the labor to apply it. (Drucker's favorite example
is the surgeon in whom these factors of production are combined.) Natural resources are necessary, of course, but taken for granted. This dif-
fers from the classical model of Ricardo and Malthus because natural resources, "the third member of the classical triad, have generally been
dropped" (Nordhaus and Tobin 1972, 14).

Mainstream Economics and the Denial of General Scarcity

Mainstream economists believe as a matter of theory and as an
inference from history that new knowledge and ingenuity can always
alleviate any natural resource shortage that may arise so that "nature
imposes particular scarcities, not an inescapable general scarcity" (Daly
1993b, 19).[6] They offer at least three arguments to support a model of
economic growth that is knowledge-dependent but not resource-limited.
According to the first of these arguments, reserves of natural resources
"themselves are actually functions of technology. The more advanced
the technology, the more reserves become known and recoverable" (Lee
1989, 116). Recent examples of reserve-increasing technologies include
the use of bacteria to leach metals from low-grade ore and the application
of computer analysis to seismic vibrations to locate oil reserves (Forbes
1994, 120).

As a result of advances of these kinds, reserves of many nonrenewable
resources have actually increased during the past decades, so that in 1993
real prices for many minerals, including fuels, stood at historical lows. Between 1987 and 1990, estimates of proven recoverable reserves of petroleum, for example, rose 11.4 percent and those of natural gas by 17.9 percent (World Resources Institute 1994, 5, 189). The 1994–95 Report from
the World Resources Institute (WRI) notes: "By a number of measures,
reserves of energy and of subsoil minerals are more abundant, and real
world prices for such commodities are generally lower today than 20 years
ago, despite rising global consumption" (5).

Second, advances in technology allow us not only to increase available reserves but also to substitute away from resources that may become scarce. When mainstream economists speak of substitutability, they generally refer to the substitution of one resource for another so that "a satisfactory substitute can always be found for the role of any one of them" (Ehrlich 1989).[7] Robert Solow (1973, 53) states this view: "Higher and rising prices of exhaustible resources lead competing producers to substitute other materials that are more plentiful and therefore cheaper." Daly (1991c, 108) correctly ascribes to economists William Nordhaus and James Tobin the view that "in the aggregate resources are infinite, that when one flow dries up, there will always be another, and that technology will always find ways to exploit the next resource."

As a result of increased efficiency and substitution away from expensive materials, prices for raw materials have not increased. Indeed, according to one authority, "virtually all minerals have experienced long-term declines in real prices during the last two generations" (Smil 1993, 57).

A third reason that many engineers, economists, and others take natural resources for granted relies on the power of technology continually to reduce the amounts of resources needed to produce a constant or increasing flow of consumer goods and services. Solow (1974, 10–11) argues, "If the future is anything like the past, there will be prolonged and substantial reductions in natural resource requirements per unit of real output."

Knowledge increases the productivity of natural resources in the same way it increases the productivity of labor. Glass fibers, for example, not only substitute for but vastly improve upon copper cables in transmitting messages. The transmission capacity of an optical fiber cable increased by an order of magnitude every four years between 1975 and 1992. Today, a thin cable using optical amplifiers and erbium-doped fibers powered by laser diode chips can carry a half million phone calls at any moment. Computers become more powerful as they grow smaller; the world's entire annual production of computer chips could fit into a single cargo plane. Energy requirements continually decrease per unit of economic output—automobiles, for example, last longer and use less steel, rubber, and fuel for each mile traveled.

Economic growth today involves pushing back the abstract frontiers of acquiring, processing, and transmitting information; it bears less and less relation to the natural resource base. In 1995, Microsoft, which has no industrial plant or product, nearly equaled IBM in market value. According to *Fortune* magazine, "For almost four years now, U.S. industry has been spending more on computers and communications equipment than on all other capital equipment combined—all the machinery needed for services, manufacturing, mining, agriculture, construction, whatever" (Huey 1994, 36).

Reflecting on these trends, the World Resources Institute (WRI) dismisses the idea that shortages of nonrenewable resources will prove a limiting factor in global economic growth. Its *1994–95 Report* states: "Even without more resource-sparing policies, . . . the cumulative effect of increasing reserves, more competition among suppliers, and technology trends that create substitutes suggests that global shortages of most nonrenewable resources are unlikely to check development in the early decades of the next century" (6).

The WRI (1994, 5) also dismisses "the frequently expressed concern that high levels of consumption will lead to resource depletion and to physical shortages that might limit growth or development opportunity." It argues that the evidence suggests, to the contrary, "that the world is not yet running out of most nonrenewable resources and is not likely to, at least in the next few decades." It is against this background that ecological economists argue that we "are now entering an era in which the limitative factor [in development] will be the remaining natural capital" (Daly 1991c, 250) and that the resource base no longer "permits economic growth to be sustained" (Daly and Townsend 1993, 9).

Ecological Economics and Resource Scarcity

Mainstream economists believe that when markets function efficiently, prices provide the best measure of the scarcity or abundance of resources relative to demand. If we accept this idea, then it would seem that the purchase of commodities for future delivery in principle provides a way to test the seriousness of predictions of impending scarcities.

Real prices for farm commodities have declined so sharply—about 40 percent since 1970—that surpluses, the bane of agricultural markets, have driven many farms out of business, erected tariffs, and impeded freer trade (World Resources Institute 1992, 97).[8] If "Cassandras" who in 1970 predicted worldwide food shortages, for example, backed up their warnings by purchasing "options" on agricultural commodities for delivery in 1994, they would have lost much of their money, since the prices of many of these commodities fell to historic lows.

Commodity price trends do not suggest that scarcities loom in the foreseeable future. With this in mind, in 1980, economic growth advocate Julian Simon challenged a group of environmentalists including Paul Ehrlich to bet on a contract for delivery ten years later of any commodities that the group chose. The Ehrlich group lost the bet. The prices of the commodities it chose (five metals) declined over ten years in both real and nominal terms; therefore, the group had to pay Simon the difference.[9]

Ehrlich stood by his belief that the price of those metals would eventually rise. He told Tierney (1990), "The bet doesn't mean anything. Julian Simon is like the guy who jumps off the Empire State Building and says how great things are going so far as he passes the 10th floor." Declining commodity prices may prove only that traders are myopic. (Had prices increased, however, some might have seen this as incontrovertible evidence of natural limits on economic growth.)

What evidence besides higher commodity prices would support the contention that resource scarcity places a "limiting factor" on growth? Is there a single resource, for example, that functions to limit production? Energy comes to mind. Oil reserves must give out sometime, even if that time is not in sight (available economically recoverable reserves are sufficient for several decades at current depletion rates),[10] and even though coal supplies at present consumption rates are sufficient for centuries, the atmosphere may not be able to handle greater emissions of carbon dioxide and other gases. Over the long run, an alternative fuel source—fusion energy, for example, or an efficient way of harnessing solar power—is likely to come into large-scale use, grounding a hydrogen-based economy.

Many ecological economists dismiss these possibilities. They believe that economic growth, by producing heat and other wastes, necessarily leads to ecological ruin. Herman Daly writes: "Even the advent of commercially viable fusion energy, . . . not only would fail to eliminate pollution constraints on economic growth, it would actually hasten humankind's progress to the brink of ecological disaster" (Daly and Townsend 1993, 9).

As this passage makes clear, no development of any kind—not even fusion energy—can falsify the fundamental thesis that economic growth is a recipe for ruin. It is true that the sun's rays furnish the planet each day with twenty thousand times the amount of energy consumed by human beings. It is also true that rapid advances in solar energy technology—for example, better photovoltaic cells and genetically engineered organisms that convert biomass to alcohol at far greater efficiencies—have encouraged many observers to believe that inexhaustible or renewable energy will soon compete in price even with cheap oil. Empirical details such as these will not affect those who know that the second law of thermodynamics entails with certainty that the economy will run out of energy. Technological advances cannot upset this law of nature.

Those who believe that the entropy law sets intractable limits on global economic growth can dismiss disagreement as ignorance or as willful stupidity. The analogy with which Ehrlich dismissed Simon—the drunk falling out the window—cannot be refuted by any evidence as the disaster is bound to come, no matter how pleasant the descent. Because no evidence can in principle refute it, this analogy has become a staple in the literature. Thus, a group of ecological economists more recently likened those with "blind faith" in technology to "the man who fell from a ten story building, and when passing the second story on the way down, concluded 'so far so good, so why not continue?'" (Folke et al. 1994, 3). No matter how well things seem to be going, the laws of nature show that disaster is only more assured. Those who fail to understand these "facts of life," as Ehrlich (1994, 41) calls them, are vulnerable to the ad hominem reply that they "believe in perpetual motion machines" and "act as if the laws of nature did not exist."

Ecological economists offer more than pessimistic predictions to back up their view that the "term 'sustainable growth' when applied to the economy is a bad oxymoron" (Daly 1993e, 267). They present at least three a priori arguments (besides the entropy law) to show that crises of pollution, depletion, and ecological breakdown must accompany and therefore abort global economic growth (Daly 1993c, 369). The first of these asserts that "natural capital [natural resources] and man-made capital are complements rather than substitutes" (Daly 1993a, 27).

The second proposes that one can speak meaningfully of the scale or size of economic activity relative to bounds set by the resource base and by the carrying capacity of biospheric systems. The recommendation then follows that we should shrink the size of the economy rather than violate natural limits.

The third argument, which ecologist Robert Goodland (1993, 7) describes as the "best evidence" that there are imminent limits to growth, relies on a constantly cited calculation by Peter Vitousek et al. that "human activity uses—directly or indirectly—about 40 percent of the net primary product of terrestrial activity today." Let us examine each of these arguments.

The Complementarity of Human and Natural Capital

In 1890, Alfred Marshall (1920) summed up the view of the classical tradition in economics by formulating a distinction between human-made capital and "natural agents . . . taken to include all free gifts of nature, such as mines, fisheries, etc." Land, in which Marshall included other natural resources, constitutes a "permanent and fixed stock while appliances made by man . . . are a flow capable of being increased or diminished." Marshall continued, "Now, if the nation *as a whole* finds its stock of planting machines or ploughs inappropriately large or inappropriately small, it can redistribute its resources. It can obtain more of that in which it is deficient, while gradually lessening its stock of such things as are superabundant: *but it cannot do that in regard to land:* it can cultivate its land more intensively but it cannot get any more." He concluded, "From the economic and from the ethical point of view, land must everywhere and always be classed as a thing by itself." [11]

In the same vein, Herman Daly (1990, 3) writes: "It must be clear to anyone . . . that material transformed and tools of transformation are complements, not substitutes. Do extra sawmills substitute for diminishing forests? Do more refineries substitute for depleted oil wells? Do larger nets substitute for declining fish populations? On the contrary, the productivity of sawmills, refineries, and fishing nets (man-made capital) will decline with the decline in forests, oil deposits, and fish." [12]

The collapse of whale stocks during the nineteenth century confirms Daly's insight that larger and more efficient fleets do not substitute for but at most complement the natural resource base. Many other examples illustrate the complementarity of natural and man-made capital. Game, for example, disappeared from Kansas and Nebraska as pioneers hunted more and more efficiently. More rifles resulted in fewer prairie hens.

Those who believe that human ingenuity can work around shortages of natural capital, however, have Edison in mind, not Ahab. When Edison invented the electric bulb, he converted whales from natural resources to aesthetic marvels and cultural icons, which they remain to this day. Pa in *Little House on the Prairie* relied on his rifle when he wanted a hen, which is the sort of example that supports Daly's thesis. But this does not limit Mr. Perdue's capacity to mass-produce chickens.

Capture fisheries are in peril, but the supply of valuable species— salmon, for example—suffers from glut owing to the excess capacity of aquaculture.[13] Fishing fleets depend on wild fisheries, but fish farming— including the prospect of direct culture of fish tissue in vitro—threatens to render both obsolete. The metals Paul Ehrlich bet on declined in price because substitutes for them were found—ceramics in place of tungsten, fiber optics in place of copper, aluminum in place of tin. The products for which eighteenth-century Americans needed forests, like masts and casks, are now primarily of antiquarian interest, since we use other materials for packaging and moving goods.

The "paperless office" is at least a possibility; in any case, no one worries about natural stocks of papyrus. This is because a plentiful resource flow, wood pulp, has replaced papyrus as the basis of paper. Genetic engineers, moreover, are improving photosynthesis and developing poplar trees that process sunlight so efficiently one can almost see them grow. As a result, the economic value of ancient forests may dwindle as their aesthetic and ethical value soars.[14]

Examples of this sort cannot confirm or disconfirm the thesis that human and natural capital are complementary. The argument is an a priori one; it asserts as a self-evident truth that "production of goods and services requires natural resources, and more production of goods and services does not provide more natural resources—it uses them up" (Daly 1993c, 370). Daly correctly identifies this thesis with "the pre-analytic conception, popular among classical economists from Malthus to Mill, that the processes of growth, both demographic and economic, are bounded by inviolable resource scarcities" (Daly and Townsend 1993, 7).[15]

On the other hand, the World Bank (1992), representing the neoclassical turn in economics, takes it as equally self-evident that human ingenuity can substitute one resource flow for another when it becomes scarce. The Bank notes: "The positive forces of substitution, technical progress, and structural change can be just as powerful as . . . inputs such as metals and minerals. . . . What matters is that the overall productivity of the accumulated capital . . . more than compensates for any loss from depletion of natural capital." The report concludes in the optative mood: "This explains why the environmental debate has rightly shifted away from concern about physical limits to . . . concern for incentives for human behavior and policies that can overcome market and policy failures" (World Bank 1992, 10, italics removed).

The Question of Scale

We cannot hope to resolve here this debate between the classical and neoclassical disciplines within economics, other than to note that it is the sort of controversy that relies heavily on intuition and in which neither side may be easily swayed by argument or by evidence. It may be more fruitful to consider, then, the larger question whether—as ecological economists contend—it makes sense to speak of the size or scale of the economy in relation to the ecological systems that contain or support it.

As one of the founders of the emerging discipline of ecological economics, Herman Daly is best known for formulating the problem of defining the optimal scale of economic activity given the carrying capacity of ecosystems (1991b, 35). Ecological economics concerns itself with the size or scale of the economy as a whole relative to the ecosystem that contains it. What is the optimal size of the economy relative to the ecological system? Herman Daly observes: "This is the big question for ecological economics" (1991a, 7).

Plainly, the concept of gross domestic product (GDP) does not give us a useful measure of the size of an economy relative to the ecological system. An economy with a small GDP, such as Poland or Albania during the communist period, may cause all sorts of ecological damage and thus be too "big" in relation to its natural environment, whereas an economy with a larger GDP, such as Sweden, may be ecologically far more benign. Daly and others present many arguments to show that GDP is not a particularly helpful measure in relating economic size to carrying ca-

pacity. "Unfortunately, current gross national product (GNP) accounting conventions conflate growth and development, counting both as
'economic growth.' We sharply distinguish between throughput growth
(growth proper) and efficiency improvement (development in the dictionary sense)" (see Goodland, Daly, and Sarafy 1992). The question arises,
then, whether there is a way to measure the size or extent of economic activity that correlates with ecological stress.

Ecological economists propose to measure the scale and growth of the
economy in terms of the physical volumes of materials that pass through
it. "*Scale*," Herman Daly (1992, 186) writes, "refers to the physical
volume of the throughput, the flow of matter-energy from the environment as low-entropy raw materials, and back to the environment as high-
entropy wastes." He adds: "Throughput is the entropic physical flow of
matter-energy from nature's sources, through the human economy and
back to nature's sinks" (1993d, 326).

This definition takes scale in a literal sense, that is, in terms of physical volume. "It is measured in absolute physical units," Daly reiterates
(Daly and Townsend 1993, 2). The scale of an economy, the amount of
"throughput" it processes, can therefore be expressed in terms of cubic
yards or "absolute physical units" of that sort. The greater the "throughput," the more weight in the "biospheric ark," thus the greater the damage to or pressure and strain on the natural environment. To achieve "sustainable development," Daly (1993e, 270) argues, the economy must stop
"at a scale at which the remaining ecosystem (the environment) can continue to function and renew itself year after year."

The problem with this argument, however, is that "throughput" or
"scale," as Daly defines it, does not seem to correlate at all with environmental stress or damage. The sheer physical volume of detergents one
uses to do laundry, for example, may be the same whether or not those
detergents contain phosphates; similarly, hair sprays that substitute a
harmless propellant for CFCs will be far more benign to the environment, even if the sheer physical volume of "throughput" is identical. An
industry that releases vast physical volumes of water vapor into the atmosphere involves huge flows of resources (water) from nature's sources
and wastes (steam) back in. Yet it may not stress the environment.

It is easy to multiply examples to show that scale, as measured in physical volumes of material throughput, has no necessary or even general

connection to ecological impact; one might cry over a gallon of spilled mercury, for instance, though not over a gallon of spilled milk. No doctor would say that every medicine or drug has the same effect if taken in the same dose. Why does Daly propose, then, that the sheer physical volume of material throughput measures potential ecological damage—without regard to what the material may be?

Presumably, Daly recognizes that some kinds of "throughput" are better or worse than others—that physical volume does not correlate with environmental stress. If so, he would then have to make all kinds of distinctions to divide the "bad" throughput from the "benign," which is to say, the kinds of "throughput" that cause environmental externalities and those that do not. This is exactly what the opposing position counsels: an ad hoc, case-by-case, regulatory approach. Thus, the concept of "throughput" or "scale" does not seem to make us conceptually better off than we were before.

"Co-opting" Nature

"Probably the best index of the scale of the human economy as a part of the biosphere," Daly writes, "is the percentage of human appropriation of the total world product of photosynthesis." Lester Brown and his colleagues similarly note: "Vitousek and his colleagues estimate that 40 percent of the earth's annual net primary production on land now goes directly to meet human needs or is indirectly used or destroyed by human activity." They add that "with people usurping an ever larger share of the earth's life-sustaining energy, natural systems will unravel faster" (Brown, Postel, and Flavin 1992, 122–23).

Daly (1993e, 268–69) makes the same point after citing Vitousek in several papers. He argues that "the human economy currently preempts one-fourth of the global net primary product of photosynthesis (NPP)." He adds that we "cannot go beyond 100 percent, and it is unlikely that we will increase NPP since the historical tendency up to now is for economic growth to reduce global photosynthesis."

This argument, which many writers present, asserts as its major premise that any increase in the size of the economy requires a proportional increase in the percentage of NPP that it "usurps." The minor premise states that it is virtually impossible to double—let us say, from

40 to 80 percent—the amount of NPP that the economy "preempts." It is impossible to double the size of the global economy, and so it is impossible to generalize American patterns and levels of consumption worldwide.

It is not obvious, however, that the amount of goods and services we produce, that is, the size of the economy, varies with the amount of NPP that we "usurp." Thus, a biotech firm that cultures cocoa in vitro need not "usurp" more NPP than the plantations that return to forest as a result. The manufacture of synthetic fibers may not "preempt" more NPP than the cotton farms and sheep ranches it puts out of business. Bio-industrial methods of production and increased yield per acre in farm-based agriculture have caused about 50 percent of cropland in America to revert to woodland or go to other uses. Californians, Israelis, and others make deserts bloom. And as for automobiles, computers, and other main-stay products of the economy, a one-to-one linear relation between economic growth and NPP "preemption" is not self-evident.

Vitousek et al. calculate that the amount of organic matter that people eat comes to less than 1 percent of NPP.[16] If one includes all terrestrial harvesting, including all forest and farm production, then one may argue that humans consume as much as 5 percent of annual NPP, mostly in renewable resources that humans plant themselves. Nevertheless, Vitousek et al. (1986, 372) "estimate that organic material equivalent to about 40 percent of the present net primary production in terrestrial ecosystems is being co-opted by human beings each year."

That this estimate is true—indeed, that it is an understatement by half—becomes clear once the term *co-opt* is defined. The authors mean "material that human beings use directly or that is used in human-dominated ecosystems by communities of organisms different from those in corresponding natural systems." They add, "People use this material directly or indirectly, it flows to different consumers and decomposers than it otherwise would, or it is lost because of human-caused changes in land use" (Vitousek et al. 1986, 370, 372).

To say that human beings co-opt NPP in this sense is only to recognize, however, that all economic activity, even that of prehistoric peoples, transforms nature. On the definition Vitousek et al. (1986) offer, human beings have co-opted terrestrial ecosystems at levels approaching 100 percent for more than five thousand years. A century ago, few, if any, undisturbed ecosystems remained on earth. The most impoverished and un-productive economies co-opt nature at least as readily as the wealthier ones. We should be living in caves today if NPP "usurpation," as Vitousek et al. define it, settled a limit on economic growth.

Daly, Brown, Goodland, and others offer no argument for their assumption of a direct linear covariance of NPP usurpation and the scale or size of an economy. Yet they rely on this assumption for the "best evidence" demonstrating "the biophysical impossibility of sustainable growth of people and their things" (Daly and Townsend 1993, 11–12).

The Difference between Nature and the Environment

The World Bank, particularly in its 1992 *World Development Report,* defends the view that economic growth (and, therefore, greater production and consumption worldwide) remains the appropriate object of development. Markets properly regulated for environmental "externalities," according to this view, are the keys to environmental improvement, provided they are accompanied by management strategies that deploy incentives as well as sound constraints (both regulatory and administrative) and seek to solve specific problems. The World Bank (1992, 36) summarizes: "The key to growing sustainably is not to produce less but to produce differently."

Although the World Bank regards economic growth as consistent with (or as required for) environmental protection, it has no illusions about its effects on nature. Economic development requires the clearing of land, draining of swamps, drilling of oil, damming of rivers, at least given the technologies of the last 200 years. Economic expansion not only "usurps," "co-opts," and "preempts" nature; it conquers, controls, supplants, and eliminates it. The World Bank acknowledges: "All economic activity transforms the natural world" (World Bank 1992, 36).

The distinction between "nature" and the "environment" does not receive enough attention. Nature is whatever humanity did not make. Something is "natural" to the extent that its qualities owe nothing to human beings. Nature is Creation, fresh from the hand of God—or, if you prefer a secular version of Genesis, it is the amazing surviving record of a billion-year-old toil of evolution. Our evolutionary and ecological heritage beggars our ability to understand or even to imagine its possibility.

Religious awe is at least as reasonable a response as scientific curiosity to the wonder of the natural world.

The values nature inspires—all of them deeply human, of course—tend to be religious, moral, and aesthetic. These ideals, judgments, and principles impel us to appreciate and to protect nature for its intrinsic qualities and not only for the uses that may benefit us. Our basic normative approach to nature, therefore, is not necessarily instrumental or even prudential. It may also be founded in religious experience, moral reflection, and aesthetic judgment. This way of valuing nature relies on arguments of principle, not prudence; it recognizes ethical more than economic constraints on growth.

The environment, in contrast to nature, comprises just those aspects of the surrounding world that are useful and that are therefore valuable for welfare-related reasons. The environment is what nature becomes when we cease to believe in it as an object of cultural, religious, and aesthetic affection and regard it wholly as a prop for our well-being—a collection of useful materials and as a sink for wastes.

The aesthetic enjoyment or appreciation of the natural environment illustrates this difference. Those who admire or appreciate nature for its intrinsic qualities value it—indeed, enjoy it—because of those qualities. They enjoy nature, then, because they value it, for example, its history, beauty, and symbolic significance. Our feelings of pleasure function cognitively; in other words, they are the faculties by which we are able to perceive what is wonderful in nature and in art. Pleasure is not the goal of the aesthetic experience; rather, it is part of our ability to experience and appreciate our surroundings.

For those who believe that only human well-being can count as a goal of public policy, in contrast, the beauty, grandeur, and symbolic significance of nature cannot be good in itself. What matters is the pleasure or "satisfaction" that these may provide human beings. From this perspective, we do not enjoy nature because we value it. Rather, we value nature because we enjoy it. Pleasure is not the means by which we appreciate; rather, it is the end we seek. These two approaches to the aesthetic experience of nature are antithetical. One locates value directly in nature. The other finds value in our experience—that is, pleasure or satisfaction—and values nature only as the cause or stimulus of that experience.

The 1992 *World Development Report* poses this question: "Environmental damage—why does it matter?" Environmental damage matters, the report concludes, because it involves "losses in health, productivity, and amenity" and therefore losses in human welfare (World Bank 1992, 45). Ecological economists would answer the question the same way. Although the debate between mainstream and ecological economists is important and profound, it should not obscure their common concern not with nature per se but exclusively with the environment.

Ecological economists favor the protection of nature because they regard it more as a benevolent mother than as a cruel adversary. Thus, although ecological economists are pessimistic about technology, they are optimistic about the utility of the natural world. They would preserve endangered plants and animals, for example, for uses that may be found for them rather than to allow normal market forces to cause mass extinctions.

What is more, they urge us to preserve the habitats of these creatures, not just specimens or tissue samples for future replication and study in vitro. The prudent or "precautionary" approach would save "all the parts," that is, whatever vestiges of nature are left. As a result, economic activity must cease doing what it usually does, which is to alter or transform nature in order to create a more hospitable environment.

"If we are to support the life-supporting capabilities of our all-important film of air, water, and soil," states "A Blueprint for Survival" (signed by thirty British scientists), "economic growth must be brought to a halt as rapidly as possible" (Ayres 1993, 191). Yet environmentalists who make these statements drive in air-conditioned cars and fly in airplanes, shop in department stores, and live in houses. They meet more often in windowless conference halls and in trendy resorts than in wilderness areas. Even they must believe that economic activity by transforming nature can and does improve the environment in which we live.

An Analogy with the Medical Sciences

The question then arises to what extent the alteration of the natural world improves and to what extent it harms the environment. The answer one gives will depend on whether one visualizes nature as a bountiful mother showering us with gifts or as a harsh mistress whose dowry is famine, pestilence, cold, and certain death. Those who assimilate nature to the Garden of Eden may believe that by returning to the way things were—by ecological restoration—we are more able to live peacefully with our surroundings and with each other. Those whose view of evolution harks back only as far as Herbert Spencer, however, might see survival more as a struggle against nature than as a search for harmony with it.

These opposing views of nature—one envisioning it as a Garden to restore, the other as a frontier to conquer—are as familiar in literature, art, biology, and religion as they are in the economic sciences. They can also be found in medicine. It is fair to say that medicine traditionally views nature as a never-ending frontier. Plague, smallpox, malaria, heart disease, and polio are all part and parcel of nature; one by one, medicine has pushed back these limits to life and is now at work on genes.

The medical sciences, whether appropriately or not, have generally adhered to the mission of altering nature whenever there is any prospect of improving any individual's well-being. This mission has led medicine to seek, whenever possible, to control nature's course, even to the point of delaying and possibly of eliminating death. Yet many medical ethicists have questioned the policy of treating patient preferences as sacrosanct.

For example, rather than seeking to extend life spans indefinitely, Daniel Callahan (1987, 223) has written that medicine should work "toward the development of an integrated perspective on a natural life span, one that knows where the boundaries are." Many medical ethicists have taken up the proposal "that we try to enter into a pervasive cultural agreement to alter our perception of death as the enemy . . . to its being instead a condition of life to be accepted."

Why should we accept death or any other "natural" limit in life—such as being short, bald, or whatever—when we may hope to alter nature, for example, to change human genetic material to our heart's desire? Why not seek a "brave new world" based on bioengineering if that is what people want?

Two kinds of reasons may come to mind. First, one might appeal to futility: We must accept natural limits—a life span of roughly four score years, for example—because nature gives us no alternative. One might eke out a few more years and then a few more—but at great social expense and with little benefit to the individual. To increase the quantity of life, in other words, we must diminish its quality. The benefits do not equal the costs.

Second, one may appeal to religious and cultural conceptions of what is morally appropriate to the human condition. Even if we could design ourselves and our children, for example, according to principles laid down in *Vogue,* this would reduce human beings to commodities. Moreover, the idea of hanging on—of making one's own generation and, therefore, its follies and prejudices permanent—appalls ethical judgment. Even if it could be, it should not be done.

Let us suppose that we could rearrange the human genome to satisfy the dreams of the most ambitious eugenicist. Everyone could then look "right," behave "well," and live indefinitely. Genetic engineers might transform or re-create nature to maximize the satisfaction of consumer preferences taken as they come, on a willingness-to-pay basis, bounded only by indifference curves between alternatives. Is this conquest of nature devoutly to be wished or feared?

With respect to nature as a whole, mainstream economists have a ready answer to this question. The conquest of nature, were it truly complete, would be an excellent thing, for this is consistent with the principle of consumer sovereignty. David Pearce (1990, 33), a prominent advocate of "green" economics, for example, argues that the only values that count in economic theory are subjective consumer preferences. He writes: "Economic values are about what people want. Something has economic value—is a benefit—if it satisfies individual preferences."

Religious ideals, moral principles, cultural convictions, and aesthetic judgments, in contrast, cannot be assimilated to preferences that people seek to satisfy to promote their own well-being. These beliefs express what people think is consistent with God's will or is right or wrong, decent or indecent, or better or worse in itself. What to do with "intrinsic" values—that is, objective moral and aesthetic judgments as distinct from subjective wants—has always baffled economists. The World Bank *Report* (1992), for example, apparently concludes that intrinsic values—not being clearly related to human welfare—are not human values. It writes: "Many people believe that things in the natural world have 'intrinsic' value separate from their value to human beings." [17]

While the state of medical ethics makes it possible to discuss the moral properties of nature in their own terms, this is not true of the economic sciences in their approach to the environment. The economic sciences regard only one thing as valuable, namely, human welfare or "utility," and cannot deal with any other way of valuing or respecting the natural world. To satisfy individual preferences is the moral course on this view—to give more people more of the goods and services they want to buy.

As technology breaks one barrier and then another—perhaps fusion and genetic engineering will carry us to yet unknown frontiers—economists have no further moral advice to offer us. Mainstream economists urge us forward as long as winners can compensate losers and still be winners; that is, if socially speaking, the benefits equal the costs. Ecological economists tell us that efforts further to transform the natural world are futile and self-defeating. Thus, we are left to argue about what we can get away with—how much natural capital remains, how much NPP we can "co-opt," and how much "throughput" will sink the biospheric ark. In environmental and ecological economics, discussion of the moral issues aside from human well-being has not yet begun.

The Most Valuable Things Are Useless

When the Pilgrims arrived in America in 1620, they encountered nature or what they called wilderness. Nature was not an Eden for them. Over the centuries, New Englanders transformed their landscape in economically rewarding ways, so that even by Thoreau's time, little if any of the original ecological fabric remained (Cronon 1983; Rap 1966). It was 100 percent "co-opted" even then. Today, vacationers, who are willing to pay more than $1,000 a week, recreate among the garden apartments, fern bars, shopping malls, boutiques, French restaurants, and marinas that stand where the Pilgrims died of famine, exposure, and disease.

Nature imposed far greater limits on the Pilgrims—who transformed it less—than it does on visitors to Plymouth today. This has happened not because humanity accepted the "constraints" and "limits" it found but precisely because it managed to lift or remove them. Fortunately, human beings, by controlling and in many instances by eradicating nature (think of the smallpox virus), have managed to develop what is known as civilization. In other words, the lessons of history suggest that the bounds of science and technology—not those of nature—constitute the ultimate limits to growth.

Unfortunately, civilization is in many respects vacuous and disappointing, especially those aspects typified by highways, condominiums, fern bars, and shopping malls. Cape Cod at the time Thoreau described it was plainly a more glorious and less tacky place than it is now. Many people know this; indeed, they go to places such as Cape Cod in search of vestiges of the natural world. They love nature, but they live in condominiums.

Economic expansion, as we have seen, tends to substitute instrumental for intrinsic value, for example, by putting Route 3 through what might otherwise have been the most breathtaking vistas of the Cape. By transforming nature into commercial environments—dells into delis, arcadias into arcades, and, in the words of the popular song, paradises into parking lots—a growing economy has created a comfortable and utilitarian environment where the Pilgrims found an inhospitable but sublime natural world.

When technology renders aspects of the environment economically obsolete, we may regard these objects—whales, for example—as belonging simply to nature. As parts of nature, they may become objects of aesthetic, moral, and religious appreciation rather than economic utility. These kinds of appreciation depend upon judgment and not necessarily desire. They express what we believe in and stand for as communities, not necessarily what we "prefer" as individuals. They have as much to do with who we are as with what we want.

The philosopher Immanuel Kant (1959, 53) formulated the relevant distinction between instrumental and intrinsic value. "That which is related to general human inclination and needs has a market price. . . . But that which . . . can be an end in itself does not have a mere relative worth, i.e., *a price,* but an intrinsic worth, i.e., *a dignity.*"

Kant also argued that aesthetic appreciation is a matter of judgment, not just preference. It is grounded in reasons, not wants. The pleasure we take in natural beauty constitutes our way of knowing or perceiving its excellence. Natural beauty is not valuable because of the pleasure it provides. Rather, that pleasure has a value—it is appropriate—because of its relation to beauty.

Environmentalists may seek to protect nature more out of love than fear, in other words, more because of its intrinsic than its economic value. Environmentalists can get only so much mileage out of predictions—some of which are thirty years old—that continued growth will "by itself bring us to a condition to self-destruct within the lifetime of our grandchildren" (Ayres 1993, 191). They may find arguments based on ethical, aesthetic, or cultural judgments to be more effective, therefore, than appeals to prudence.

It will take a sea-change in perspective, however, for economists to suspect that natural objects may have intrinsic—that is to say, religious, aesthetic, and moral—dignity rather than simply an instrumental or market price.[18] Today, neither mainstream nor ecological economists show any interest in the idea that nature might be protected for its objective aesthetic qualities, its bewildering majesty, or its moral and religious significance. Instrumental value—the relevance of nature to long-term welfare—is all that seems to matter to either side. And neither will understand you when you say that all the most valuable things are quite useless.

NOTES

1. Ehrlich (1974, 48) also wrote that at the 1973 world consumption rate, proven reserves of oil would last just slightly more than thirty-five years (that is, until 2009).

2. This assertion, although plausible, needs more defense than Daly has given. Rather than leave it as an intuitive truth, we must show it to be true in respect to particular processes. Here opposition is to be expected: some scientists believe, for example, that the greenhouse effect will be a gradual process.

3. Herman Daly (1994, 28) writes: "The world is moving from an era when man-made capital was the limiting factor into an era in which remaining natural capital is the limiting factor" (italics removed).

4. Stiglitz commenting on Solow 1956.

5. Stiglitz referring to Solow 1957.

6. Daly is citing H. J. Barnett and C. Morse, *Scarcity and Growth: The Economics of Natural Resource Availability* (Baltimore: Johns Hopkins University Press, 1963), 11.

7. Ehrlich quotes Barnett and Morse, *Scarcity and Growth*, 11.

8. See also Gugliotta 1993.

9. In October 1980, Paul Ehrlich and colleagues John Harte and John Holdren accepted a public offer by Julian Simon to let anyone pick any natural resource—grain, oil, coal, metals, timber, etc.—and any future date. If the price of the commodities rose in real terms by the date, Simon would pay the difference; if they fell, he would receive the difference. The parties drew up a futures contract obligating Simon to sell to the Ehrlich group in 1990 a basket of five metals—chrome, copper, nickel, tin, and tungsten—at 1980 prices ($1,000). Each of the metals, when adjusted for inflation, declined in price. The *New York Times Magazine* reported that the prices dropped so sharply

that Simon would have come out ahead even without the inflation adjustment called for in the bet. Tierney (1990, 52) commented: "For many uses, the metals were replaced by cheaper materials. . . . Telephone calls went through satellites and fiber-optic lines instead of copper wires. Ceramics replaced tungsten in cutting tools," and so on.

Daniel B. Luten (1988) described Simon's offer as a "sucker bet." The reason is inflation: "You cannot win unless prices rise faster than the interest rate." Luten neglected to mention that Simon adjusted prices for inflation, and the price overall declined in nominal as well as real terms. Oddly, Luten imagined that Simon would hold and earn interest on the money wagered, but this was not part of the bet, since it involved only a payment at the end of the period.

10. According to Holdren (1992, 165), reserves of oil and natural gas will last 70–100 years, if exploited at 1990 rates. (This does not include even larger deposits of oil shale, heavy oils, and unconventional sources of gas.) Holdren adds that at 1990 consumption rates, there is at least a 1,500-year supply of coal. He concludes that "running out of energy resources in any global sense is not what the energy problem is all about."

The World Bank (1992, 115) estimated that fossil fuel reserves are more than 600 times the present rate of extraction. The Bank concluded that "fears that the world may be running out of fossil fuels are unfounded."

11. For a good discussion on the views of Marshall—who is often regarded as the father of neoclassical economics—with respect to land as a factor in production, see Salah El Serafy, "The Environment as Capital," in *Ecological Economics: The Science and Management of Sustainability*, ed. Robert Costanza (New York: Columbia University Press, forthcoming), 168–75.

Marshall here echoes David Ricardo, who formulated the economic theory of rent earlier that century. Ricardo saw that as population grows, wages and capital will end up as rent paid to those who own the best "fixed" factors of production, especially if they erect tariffs (for example, the Corn Laws) against imports. Ricardo noted that improvements in technology can brake the tendency of owners of the best land to absorb as "rents" the difference between their cost and that of the least efficient producer of food and other goods. The tendency of prices to rise as more marginal lands enter production "is happily checked at repeated intervals by the improvements in machinery, connected with the production of necessaries, as well as by the discoveries in the science of agriculture." See David Ricardo, *The Works and Correspondence*, ed. Pierro Sraffa (Cambridge: Cambridge University Press, 1951–55), 1:120.

12. Critics of this view compare it with that of William Stanley Jevons, who predicted in 1865 that the British economy and population would have to shrink

enormously given the impending exhaustion of coal reserves and the "impossibility of finding a substitute." See W. S. Jevons, *The Coal Question,* ed. A. W. Flux (London: Macmillan, 1906).

13. Norway's immense salmon farming industry produced about 150,000 tons in 1989 and earned $1.35 billion. Similarly rising production in Scotland, Canada, Maine, and elsewhere has caused world prices to fall. In the resulting trade war, the U.S. maintains a 26 percent duty on Norwegian salmon.

    For discussion, see Caroline E. Mayer, "Caught Up in a Salmon Rivalry: Norway's Imports Stalled by Maine's Fish Farmers," *Washington Post,* 14 April 1991, E1.

14. According to T. M. Powledge (1984), biotechnology will have its greatest effect on the way wood and other forest commodities are produced. "Forestry will probably realize the greatest improvement of any crop from biotechnology."

    Larry Tombaugh, a forest economist at Michigan State University, adds that genetic engineering, moreover, can compensate for the native species that are lost when forests fall to the chainsaw and axe. Native genetic material not only can be preserved in gene "banks" but also can be manipulated, varied, and improved in endless ways. "This requires genetic manipulation to evolve vigorous and fast-growing trees with a short reproductive cycle which can be mass propagated" (Powledge 1984, 763).

15. These classical economists, according to the commentator Paul Christensen, based their pessimism partly on the a priori doctrine that natural and human-made resources are complementary, not substitutable. He notes that even Adam Smith divided capital into two complementary categories: fixed (which included land) and circulating (which included technology or machines). Christensen summarizes: "Manufacturing, it was recognized, was a materials-processing activity that obeys the law of conservation of mass. Manufactured products require material inputs, labor, tools or machines, and the energetic materials required by the laborers and other engines. Thus, an increase in output in manufacturing requires a proportional increase in raw materials." See Paul Christensen, "Driving Forces, Increasing Returns, and Ecological Sustainability," in *Ecological Economics: The Science and Management of Sustainability,* ed. Robert Costanza (New York: Columbia University Press, forthcoming), 77.

16. To determine how many petagrams (Pg) of organic matter people directly eat (or need to eat), the authors multiplied 5 billion people by 2,500 kilocalories/person to yield on conversion 0.91 Pg of organic material—less than 1 percent of their estimated total NPP, 131.1 Pg.

17. The Bank adopts explicitly a moral theory that is entirely welfarist and subjective. Values are assimilated to preferences that individuals seek to satisfy

in order to enhance their own welfare as they see it. The Bank acknowledges that "many people believe that other living things in the natural world have an 'intrinsic' value separate from their value to human beings." Thus the Bank divides neatly and exclusively between preferences that people seek to satisfy to benefit themselves and values that are "separate from human beings" (*World Development Report 1992*, 45).

The most urgent values that motivate us with respect to nature, however, are deeply human values that are not based in human welfare. Many people believe, for example, that God created nature, and this gives us a sufficient reason to respect it. Religious beliefs and values of this kind are hardly "separate from human beings," since religion is the most intimate expression of human reflection on the meaning and origin of life. Reflections or beliefs of this kind constitute values "separate from human beings" only in the sense that they are not subjective self-interested welfare-seeking preferences. The Bank apparently associates only preferences of that kind with values that have anything to do with human beings.

18. The distinction between instrumental and intrinsic value—like that between the environment and nature—does not receive sufficient attention. Consider the example of children. Worldwide, children are often treated as economic resources. Whether sold as prostitutes, owned as slaves, or simply sent out to earn wages in the fields or mines, children may be valued wholly for their instrumental or marketable properties. At the end of the nineteenth century, over a million children in America labored in sweatshops or "hurried" coal in mines.

All of us believe, of course, that children, being persons, should be cherished for their own sake rather than allocated to the highest bidder. The reasons to respect children are primarily moral rather than instrumental, prudential, or economic. Likewise, we may cherish many aspects of nature for their intrinsic properties rather than for any benefit we may hope to obtain from them. Many of us who seek to preserve magnificent ecosystems such as rain forests, for example, treasure the intrinsic qualities of the play of life they contain. We do not rely on conjectures about the instrumental value of these climax ecosystems—for example, that they add to global oxygen budgets or harbor organisms that could cure rather than cause disease.

REFERENCES

Ayres, Robert U. 1993. "Cowboys, Cornucopians, and Long-Run Sustainability." *Ecological Economics* 8:189–297.

Barnett, H. J., and C. Morse. 1963. *Scarcity and Growth: The Economics of Natural Resource Availability*. Baltimore: Johns Hopkins University Press.

Boulding, Kenneth. 1993. "The Economics of the Coming Spaceship Earth." In *Valuing the Earth: Economics, Ecology, Ethics,* ed. Herman E. Daly and Kenneth N. Townsend, 297–309. Cambridge: MIT Press.

Brown, Lester R., Sandra Postel, and Christopher Flavin. 1992. "From Growth to Sustainable Development." In *Population, Technology, and Lifestyle: The Transition to Sustainability,* ed. Robert Goodland, Herman E. Daly, and Salah El Serafy, 119–127. Washington, D.C.: Island Press.

Callahan, Daniel. 1987. *Setting Limits: Medical Goals in an Aging Society.* New York: Simon and Schuster.

Costanza, Robert, Herman E. Daly, and Joy A. Bartholomew. 1991. "Goals, Agenda, and Policy Recommendations for Ecological Economics." In *Ecological Economics: The Science and Management of Sustainability,* ed. Robert Costanza, 1–20. New York: Columbia University Press.

Cronon, William. 1983. *Changes in the Land: Indians, Colonists, and the Ecology of New England.* New York: Hill and Wang.

Daly, Herman E. 1985. "Moving to a Steady-State Economy." In *The Cassandra Conference: Resources and the Human Predicament,* ed. Paul R. Ehrlich and John P. Holdren, 271–85. College Station: Texas A&M Press.

———. 1990. "Toward Some Operational Principles of Sustainable Development." *Ecological Economics* 2:1–6.

———. 1991a. "Ecological Economics and Sustainable Development: From Concept to Policy." Divisional Working Paper No. 1991–24. Washington, D.C.: World Bank, Environment Department.

———. 1991b. "Elements of Environmental Macroeconomics." In *Ecological Economics: The Science and Management of Sustainability,* ed. Robert Costanza, 32–46. New York: Columbia University Press.

———. 1991c. *Steady State Economics.* 2d ed. Washington, D.C.: Island Press.

———. 1992. "Allocation, Distribution, and Scale: Towards an Economics That Is Efficient, Just, and Sustainable." *Ecological Economics* 6:185–93.

———. 1993a. "From Empty World Economics to Full-World Economics: Recognizing an Historical Turning Point in Economic Development." In *Population, Technology, and Lifestyle: The Transition to Sustainability,* ed. Robert Goodland, Herman E. Daly, and Salah El Serafy, 23–37. Washington, D.C.: Island Press.

———. 1993b. "Introduction to *Essays toward a Steady-State Economy.*" In *Valuing the Earth: Economics, Ecology, Ethics,* ed. Herman E. Daly and Kenneth N. Townsend, 11–47. Cambridge: MIT Press.

———. 1993c. Postscript: Some Common Misunderstandings and Further Issues Concerning a Steady-State Economy. In *Valuing the Earth: Economics, Ecology, Ethics,* ed. Herman E. Daly and Kenneth N. Townsend, 365–82. Cambridge: MIT Press.

————. 1993d. "The Steady-State Economy: Toward a Political Economy of Bio-physical Equilibrium and Moral Growth." In *Valuing the Earth: Economics, Ecology, Ethics,* ed. Herman E. Daly and Kenneth N. Townsend, 325–63. Cambridge: MIT Press.

————. 1993e. "Sustainable Growth: An Impossibility Theorem." In *Valuing the Earth: Economics, Ecology, Ethics,* ed. Herman E. Daly and Kenneth N. Townsend, 267–74. Cambridge: MIT Press.

————. 1994. "Operationalizing Sustainable Development by Investing in Natural Capital." In *Investing in Natural Capital,* ed. AnnMari Jansson et al., 22–37. Washington, D.C.: Island Press.

Daly, Herman E., and Kenneth Townsend. 1993. Introduction to *Valuing the Earth: Economics, Ecology, Ethics,* ed. Herman E. Daly and Kenneth N. Townsend, 1–12. Cambridge: MIT Press.

Drucker, Peter. 1993. *Post Capitalist Society.* New York: Harper Business.

Ehrlich, Paul R. 1989. "The Limits to Substitution: Meta-Resource Depletion and a New Economic-Ecological Paradigm." *Ecological Economics* 1:9–16.

————. 1994. "Ecological Economics and the Carrying Capacity of the Earth." In *Investing in Natural Capital: The Ecological Economics Approach to Sustainability,* ed. AnnMari Jansson et al., 38–56. Washington, D.C.: Island Press.

Ehrlich, Paul R., and Anne H. Ehrlich. 1974. *The End of Affluence.* New York: Ballantine Books.

Folke, Carl, Monica Hammer, Robert Costanza, and AnnMari Jansson. 1994. "Investing in Natural Capital—Why, What, and How?" In *Investing in Natural Capital: The Ecological Economics Approach to Sustainability,* ed. AnnMari Jansson et al., 1–20. Washington, D.C.: Island Press.

Forbes. 1994. "Seeing into the Earth." 20 June, 77:120.

Goodland, Robert. 1993. "The Case That the World Has Reached Limits." In *Population, Technology, and Lifestyle: The Transition to Sustainability,* ed. Robert Goodland, Herman E. Daly, and Salah El Serafy, 3–22. Washington, D.C.: Island Press.

Goodland, Robert, Herman E. Daly, and Salah El Sarafy. 1992. Introduction to *Population, Technology, and Lifestyle: The Transition to Sustainability,* xi–xvi. Washington, D.C.: Island Press.

Gugliotta, Guy. 1993. "World Bank: Ranks of Hungry Can Be Halved." *Washington Post,* 30 November, A22, C1.

Holdren, John. 1992. "The Energy Predicament in Perspective." In *Confronting Climate Change,* ed. I. Mintzer, 163–69. New York: Cambridge University Press.

Huey, John. 1994. "Waking Up to the New Economy." *Fortune,* 27 June, 36–46.

Jansson, AnnMari, M. Hammer, Carl Folke, and Robert Costanza. 1994. *Invest-*

ing in Natural Capital: The Ecological Economics Approach to Sustainability, 1–20. Washington, D.C.: Island Press.

Kant, Immanuel. 1959. *Foundations of the Metaphysics of Morals.* Edited by Robert Wolf, translated by Lewis W. Beck. Indianapolis: Bobbs-Merrill.

Lee, Thomas H. 1989. "Advanced Fossil Fuel Systems and Beyond." In *Technology and Environment,* ed. Jesse H. Ausubel and Hedy E. Sladovich, 114–36. Washington, D.C.: National Academy Press.

Luten, Daniel B. 1988. "Energy and Material Resources." In *The Cassandra Conference: Resources and the Human Predicament,* ed. Paul R. Ehrlich and John P. Holdren, 101–10. College Station: Texas A&M University Press.

Marshall, Alfred. 1920. *Principles of Economics.* 8th ed. London: Macmillan.

Meadows, Donella H., Dennis L. Meadows, and Jorgen Randers. 1992. *Beyond the Limits.* Post Hills, Vt.: Chelsea Green.

Nordhaus, William B., and James Tobin. 1972. "Is Growth Obsolete?" In *Economic Growth,* ed. National Bureau of Economic Research, 1–80. New York: Columbia University Press.

Pearce, David. 1990. "Environmental and Economic Values." In *Towards an Ecologically Sustainable Society,* ed. Britt Aniansson and Uno Svedin, 33–34. Stockholm: Swedish Council for Planning Coordination of Research (FRN).

Powledge, T. M. 1984. "Biotechnology Touches the Forest." *Bio/Technology* 2:763–72.

Rap, Hugh M. 1966. "The View from John Anderson's Farm: A Perspective on the Use of Land." *Forest History* 9 (April): 2–11.

Schelling, Thomas. 1992. "Some Economics of Global Warming." *American Economic Review* 82 (March): 1–14.

Smil, Vacliv. 1993. *Global Ecology: Environmental Change and Social Flexibility.* London: Routledge.

Solow, Robert M. 1956. "A Contribution to the Theory of Economic Growth." *Quarterly Journal of Economics* 70:65–94.

———. 1957. "Technical Change and the Aggregate Production Function." *Review of Economics and Statistics* 39:312–20.

———. 1970. *Growth Theory: An Exposition.* New York: Oxford University Press.

———. 1973. "Is the End of the World at Hand?" In *The Economic Growth Controversy,* ed. Andrew Weintraub et al., 38–61. New York: International Arts and Sciences Press.

———. 1974. "The Economics of Resources or the Resources of Economics." *American Economic Review* 64 (May): 1–14.

Stiglitz, Joseph E. 1990. "Comments: Some Retrospective Views on Growth Theory." In *Growth, Productivity, Unemployment,* ed. Peter Diamond, 50–67. Cambridge: MIT Press.

Tierney, John. 1990. "Betting on the Planet." *New York Times Magazine,* 2 December, sec. 6.

Vitousek, Peter M., Paul R. Ehrlich, Anne H. Ehrlich, and Pamela Matson. 1986. "Human Appropriation of the Products of Photosynthesis." *BioScience* 36:368–73.

World Bank. 1992. *World Development Report 1992: Development and the Environment.* New York: Oxford University Press.

World Resources Institute. 1994. *World Resources 1994–95.* New York: Oxford University Press.

World Resources Institute in collaboration with the United Nations Environmental Program and the United Nations Development Program. 1992. *World Resources 1992–93: A Guide to the Global Environment.* New York: Oxford University Press.

JAN WILLEM BOL

Challenging Business Education

The Environment, Ethics, and . . . ?

Faced with unparalleled environmental constraints, many business, government, and environmental organizations are encouraging business schools to develop visions of a "new and improved" curriculum. These developmental efforts attempt to integrate certain implications of current world environmental conditions into business curricula and aim at replacing the "business as usual" paradigm with a significantly different worldview. This, in turn, necessitates the incorporation of dimensions previously not included in traditional business education. This chapter will identify some of these developmental efforts and briefly look at how these curricular innovations are being adopted by schools of business.

Traditionally, business schools have focused on helping future leaders achieve a high degree of competency in a variety of functional areas, such as accounting, marketing, and finance. The resulting level of "vocational expertise," along with other factors, has contributed to the attainment of unprecedented levels of economic development in many western societies. Yet arguably the foundational ethic of such an educational orientation implicitly discourages critical examination of the results of prevailing corporate decision-making practices and, if warranted, the identification and implementation of alternative, value-based decision-making approaches.

An argument also will be made that other subjects are waiting in the wings for business schools to deal with. The pattern presented by all these subjects (the environment, ethics, etc.) suggests a need for fundamental changes in the raison d'être of business education and, consequently, the means by which professional business people will be taught in the future. A number of radically different pedagogical approaches and experiences will be discussed briefly.

The Current State of Affairs in Business Education

Ever since Joseph Wharton contributed $100,000 toward the establishment of a curriculum for professional business education at the University of Pennsylvania in 1881, the number of business students who have graduated from U.S. business schools has grown steadily. In 1919 there were 48 business programs, which grew to 587 in 1956. During the 1919–20 academic year, 1,576 bachelor of business degrees were awarded (110 master's degrees), which grew to 50,000 bachelor of business degrees (5,205 master's degrees) during the 1957–58 academic year, representing 13 percent of all university degrees (Gordon and Howell 1959). During the past four decades this growth in business education continued. In some universities as many as one-third of all students major in business, and an MBA degree continues to be one of the more desired degrees (presumably driven, in part, by the high starting salaries of some graduating students).

To ensure minimum, yet consistent, quality standards across business schools, the American Assembly of Collegiate Schools of Business (AACSB) was created in 1916 (Dirksen 1966). In spite of the standards developed and enforced by the AACSB, reports (such as those published by the Carnegie Corporation and the Ford Foundation in 1959) observed that schools had become too lax in educating business students about broader social and political issues. For example, although accredited business schools were required to make sure that business students received at least 40 percent of their business education outside business, too many students were not receiving sufficient exposure to the humanities (Gordon and Howell 1959). In response to the need to expose students to broader issues, many business schools subsequently added a business law course to their curricula to deal with legal, social, and economic issues.

The societal turmoil of the sixties reinforced the need to broaden the business curriculum, and in 1967 the AACSB required business programs to cover not only legal and economic issues but also social and political issues. In 1974 this requirement was expanded to include ethical considerations. In response, many business schools developed a business and society course. By the early nineties, about two thirds of all accredited business schools offered a business and society course. Of these schools two thirds required students to take the course and the remaining one third offered the course as an elective (Collins and Wartick 1995). Business ethics, either as a separate course or as a component of the business and society course, enjoyed particular growth during the eighties and early nineties.

A number of observations can be made with respect to the efforts of many business schools to broaden their business curricula. First, business and society courses seem to suffer somewhat from an identity crisis, in that they have become the catch-all course where such issues as ethics and the environment are brought together (often because it appears impossible to integrate them fully into the existing curriculum). Second, a 1990 study updating the state of affairs in business and society courses across business schools revealed that none of the faculty teaching business and society courses were formally trained in environmental science issues, and many did not appear to have any significant or formal training in ethics, either.[1] Last, it appears that the approaches most business schools have taken over the last few decades to include broader business issues have left many programs without a clear holistic and integrated curriculum. It will be equally difficult in the future to incorporate emerging topics into the already overloaded and fragmented business curriculum.

The Current State of the Environment

How important is it to include environmental issues into the business curriculum? And, if found to be significant, where in the business curriculum should environmental issues be integrated?

Elsewhere in this book, the current state of the environment is discussed. In addition, most contemporary management textbooks and journals are replete with detailed accounts of the most significant environmental conditions that have a direct bearing on corporations and their decision-making processes (see, for example, Kolluru 1994). To offer another account of these conditions appears unwarranted. It is argued here that most authors of relevant business texts and articles are in general agreement about the necessity to consider at least the environment as an important stakeholder in any corporate decision. Furthermore, agreeing to include the environment as a stakeholder without further elaboration does not preempt additional scientific debate on the causes of ozone depletion or the effects of CFCs on global warming. In spite of recently published data about these issues, the controversies concerning the appropriateness of certain methodologies to identify the causes and results of environmental degradation are important, yet beyond the scope and meaning of this article. Moreover, although the exact relationships may not have been conclusively established, the scientific debate on the causes of environmental degradation is reminiscent of the seemingly endless debate on the link between smoking and lung cancer. Most people would simply accept the existence of a causal relationship without a need to belabor the scientific intricacies.

Thus, assuming general agreement about the need to include the environment in business education, and given the fact that most business curricula appear to be overloaded and in need of a more holistic design, business educators need to evaluate the future goals, approaches, and contents of their entire educational offering. A brief look at the nature of what the twenty-first-century manager will look like may offer insight into these educational requirements.

Training the Twenty-first-Century Manager

The nature and significance of global environmental conditions arguably necessitate the redefinition of raison d'être of business. Merely to add environmental issues to the "business as usual" agenda would ignore the ramifications of global environmental conditions for business and how business administration is being taught.

There are at least three tasks to be carried out to determine what the twenty-first-century manager will need in terms of business education. First, borrowing the concept of "Right Livelihood" from Buddhist traditions (see Whitmyer 1994), which suggest a number of key values by which a Buddhist ought to live his/her life, I suggest that any redesign of business education should start with a redefinition of "Right Corporate Livelihood." This would detail the values underlying a rewarding and sustainable coexistence between a corporation and the environment in such a way as to maintain the general integrity of ecosystems.

Second, based on the definition of "Right Corporate Livelihood," an assessment will have to be made of the knowledge and skills necessary to establish and maintain a corporate culture that aims at achieving the inherent goals and values of sustainability. For example, if sustainability of both the environment and corporate livelihood is to be achieved, what scientific, economic, and knowledge skills does the twenty-first-century manager need to support this new corporate philosophy?

Finally, business educators must decide if and how these skills can be taught and what structural and content changes will need to be made to the entire business program. A review of the relevant literature suggests a great deal of agreement on what is needed, although the task of how to go about it hints at general confusion in both academic and corporate circles (see, for instance, Orr 1995). In the past, the underlying themes of business education stressed the importance of tools and techniques by which companies could dominate their markets and pursue self-interest and independence, while stressing short-term, quantitative results. This "mechanistic" philosophy starkly contrasts with a more holistic, organic approach to business, which stresses interdependence, long-term, qualitative, and communal thinking.

These latter values, when integrated into an educational curriculum, will allow business students to become "integrators," "system thinkers," "cross-disciplinarians," "synthesizers," "critical evaluators," "stewards," and "logicians," rather than the "vocational experts" referred to before. The latter would need instruction in tools, techniques, and fundamental theories, something many business schools have perfected over the previous decades.

In short, the new breed of managers would require a fundamentally different educational experience, one that aims at developing a significantly different way of thinking and acting. Indeed, a business student may well need to become more of an anthropologist, social theorist, economist, philosopher, theologian, and environmentalist, as compared with a marketer, accountant, or financial analyst. Clearly, this will necessitate including subjects that previously have not been considered part of business education's domain. We will come back to this later.

The redefinition of the raison d'être of business will force business schools to accept a much broader definition of its general discipline, thereby focusing more on the teaching of an inquiry into the way business ought to work, given environmental and other concerns. In doing so, business education will be more likely to withstand the test of time rather than finding itself repeatedly responding to changing conditions that, as we have seen, result in a fragmented and confusing business curriculum. Certainly, to bring about such fundamental changes will be scary and intimidating and will require not only a great deal of leadership from the academy, business, and students, but also a healthy dose of humility.

Achieving Transformation

How can business education achieve this transformation, and are there examples of business schools that are already changing their curricula to include this broader philosophy of business?

A nonexhaustive scan of some of the reported accounts of business schools that are integrating environmental issues into their curricula suggests at least three ways by which this may be achieved. First, many schools seem to prefer an evolutionary approach by adding an elective on environmental issues into their core curriculum. Others have chosen to collaborate with centers or institutes in environmental studies (on or off campus) and then to develop jointly a program of new modules or courses—even university degrees. A final group of "revolutionaries" appears to envision an altogether different business curriculum and is creating vastly different programs and even business schools. Here are a few examples from each category.

Some of the leading business schools in the United States are developing elective courses in environmental issues. These courses, often taught by existing faculty who take a personal and professional interest in this area, usually are not required and deal with issues such as how to include the environment when making marketing, financial, or managerial decisions. This approach integrates environmental issues throughout existing courses by faculty who are willing to devote one or more class periods to discuss, for example, the need to eliminate CFCs in a particular production process and the way a company may go about developing, testing, and implementing alternatives.

In order to deal successfully with these issues in existing courses, faculty will need resources, such as cases, articles, references, etc. The Management Institute for Environment and Business (MEB) in Washington, D.C. offers business schools a ready-made approach to assess the need to "environmentalize" their curricula, as well as an extensive library of relevant materials that faculty can adopt. Given that most business schools are experiencing budgetary constraints and lack of faculty resources, MEB's help and expertise are welcome resources that can "jump-start" the effort to move forward. MEB has assisted many of the leading business schools, including Northwestern University, New York University, University of Michigan, and University of Texas–Austin.

What is particularly appealing to these business schools is that this approach to effect change is likely to fit best into its current curricular philosophy and therefore will not challenge or upset already fragile and "tested" curriculum committees, faculty, and administrators. Therein, however, also lies the main disadvantage of this "evolutionary" approach. Simply to add more electives within existing programs is not likely to bring about the fundamental changes that really are needed. Good intentions notwithstanding, this approach also does not show evidence of developing a more holistic or integrated business curriculum, which only exacerbates the identity crisis from which most overloaded and fragmented business curricula seem to suffer.

A second group of business schools have attempted to address the disadvantages of the "evolutionary" approach by developing joint ventures between various resources on or off campus. Aimed at bringing about more profound changes, these schools have set out on a course of activities that potentially can change the nature of business education within the existing "infrastructure" of their academic institutions. Two examples will suffice.

The Corporate Environmental Management Program (CEMP) at the University of Michigan is a truly collaborative effort between the university's school of natural resources and environment and the business school. In an attempt to cross disciplinary boundaries, the CEMP program was created to become a "third" entity, located "between" the two colleges, that trains executives and students to become leaders in economically and environmentally sustainable organizations. Students can enroll in a three-year program and be exposed to both management methods and environmental science and, upon graduation, receive an MBA and a master's degree of environmental studies. Thus, environmental issues are part of an integrated, holistic approach to provide state-of-the-art business education and are not merely added on to an existing business program.

Miami University (Ohio) also has formed a joint venture on campus. At its inception, six faculty, three from the natural sciences and three from the business disciplines, established the Miami University Sustainability Project (MUSP). They have developed an undergraduate capstone course, one of a number of capstone courses from which seniors have to choose in order to graduate. The course, "Sustainability Perspectives in Resources and Business," integrates key scientific and environmental theories and concepts with management philosophies and practices. For example, students are exposed to the concept of sustainability, systems issues, valuation procedures, environmental ethics, corporate planning and policy, and environmental security and policy issues. Throughout the course, students are asked to apply these principles in a series of cases developed specifically for this course and designed to demonstrate the complexities of environmental management. Students are challenged to provide realistic answers to problems caused by declining quantities of critical resources and growing public awareness of environmental health risks. They are confronted with the disparities between business and scientific views of resource use, waste disposal, risk, and the consumer society. The course description indicates that students will be required to "think critically about (1) how the best scientific knowledge can be used in evaluating resource use options; (2) the parameters of business planning, ethics, and profitability; and (3) the role and impact of citizens, human values, and government or corporate institutions in policymaking."

Both the CEMP and the MUSP programs attempt to effect considerable change in business education from within the academy. In addition, these collaborative efforts are aimed at transcending disciplinary boundaries and seem to establish an integrated and more holistic business curriculum. These efforts are undeniably resource-consuming and hard to bring about. Also, the results are likely to cause structural changes to the business curriculum and therefore will require flexibility, resources, and support from university administrations. Clearly, these requirements will make this approach less attractive to most business schools, in spite of the fact that the resulting programmatic innovations are likely to bring about more profound changes than those achieved by a more "evolutionary" approach.

The third example of an even more "revolutionary" effort is the New Academy of Business at Dartington (England), a collaborative arrangement involving The Body Shop and Schumacher College, both located in England. An international organization marketing cosmetics, The Body Shop claims to integrate environmental, social, economic, and spiritual values throughout its business practices. Schumacher College, named after economist E. F. Schumacher, offers courses designed to explore the fundamental problems now facing the world in order to define the foundations of a more balanced and harmonious worldview. This, in turn, will help define a corporate philosophy that aims at achieving economic and environmental sustainability.

Courses in science, ecology, economics, spirituality, or the humanities are part of the new curriculum at the New Academy of Business, and students may obtain a master's degree in socially responsible business or a master's degree in new paradigm business. Although the curriculum is not part of, or affiliated with, a traditional business school program, it is hoped that business schools around the world will accept the legitimacy of the program and allow their students to spend a semester for credit. The program was developed with the help of the World Business Academy (United States) and the Social Venture Network (Europe), two organizations working to develop and implement socially conscious business practices.

Finally, new technologies such as teleconferencing and the Internet are supporting the development of the "Virtual University." No longer bound by the need to be in the same location, "centers of knowledge" now can be connected electronically and expose students to a variety of otherwise unavailable resources. For example, a renowned expert in ecosystems who happens to be located, say, in Japan can become part of an international "consortium" that teaches via electronic means to a number of business students at universities or companies around the globe. Such innovations create a multitude of possibilities to teach business in a wholly different way, although the advance of technology, in and of itself, does not imply necessarily that the content and structure of the business curriculum will change accordingly.

However, these new technologies do provide the opportunity to link people and places in ways that previously had been impossible. In doing so, faculty are free to redesign their courses and include topics and areas of interest that they had not been able to cover before. Given that additional talent and resources are available, faculty may choose to invite distant colleagues or business people to be part of their "electronic course," much like the guest speakers who used to come to their classes in person.

The above cited two examples of "revolutionary" changes to business education are based on a significantly different worldview, one driven primarily by a critical assessment of current global needs. This evaluation has convinced those pursuing this approach that other, less radical efforts to redesign business programs will not bring about the kinds of fundamental changes critical for sustaining economic and environmental integrity. Effecting change within traditional business education is attempted from outside universities with the help of different and often unlikely partners. In the absence of established academic practices and institutions (such as a nine-month calendar, faculty who need and want to be tenured, administrators who do not promote or reward pedagogical changes, and so on), these innovators are free to develop new programs from the ground up. This process may yield a different approach to business education, one that, these innovators hope, will encourage a rather status quo–oriented academy of business educators to develop the next generation of business programs.

Few business schools, however, are in a position to allocate the resources to evaluate and subsequently implement such fundamental changes. Apart from the visionary leadership that is a necessary condition to this level of change, faculty must be willing and be encouraged to research, learn, and integrate new concepts, views, and theories. With the exception of the above-mentioned institutions, only a handful of business schools have made some level of commitment to examining the possibility of fundamental change to their curricula. But even such a pledge is no guarantee of institutional reform. For example, a major East Coast business school announced that it would allocate significant resources to this effort as long as its main method of instruction (in this instance, cases) was not to be affected. Similarly, the author attempted for two years to introduce an environmental management course at a major midwestern business school that had access to a world-renowned, on-campus institute for environmental studies. Notwithstanding the considerable efforts of the director of the institute, the business school, pressured by significant budgetary constraints, entrenched divisional boundaries, and a commitment to (and rewarding of) "conventional" research and teaching, never embraced the potential to differentiate itself from other business schools it was competing with increasingly unsuccessfully (the University of Michigan being one of them).

In developing management programs, business schools often rely on inputs from business leaders. It may therefore not be surprising that the growth in environmental education in business schools may parallel the growth of corporations' sustainable strategies. As Hart (1997) points out, not many organizations have fully embraced both the need for and the understanding of corporate sustainable strategies and that some leap of faith may be warranted to move toward such efforts. Presumably the same can be recommended to business school administrations and faculties.

Conclusion

These three approaches to changing business education all have advantages and disadvantages. Some schools of business may find one method more appealing, and others may prefer combining aspects of two or three approaches. For example, the University of Michigan is developing the "Virtual University" within CEMP, and Miami University's MUSP program is pursuing the establishment of a permanent Center for Sustainability that will have university-wide curricular responsibilities across presently defined divisional boundaries.

Notwithstanding these innovative and significant efforts, however well intentioned, any attempt merely to include environmental awareness within business education will bring about only superficial effects that are unlikely to produce the desired changes in the way students think and behave once they become corporate managers.

To teach business students the ins and outs of pollution prevention, how to reduce waste, or how to recycle materials will not address the fundamental issues identified above. Business education must be willing to address the moral significance of, say, the fact that it takes 300–500 gallons of water to raise one pound of beef, or the futility of reducing the amount of packaging of an essentially useless product. As Gladwin points out (1993), "Greening represents a necessary but not a sufficient condition for sustainable development." Poverty alleviation, population sta-bilization, and a more equal distribution of resources and costs must be dealt with within the business curriculum. These are the real issues for humanity, and thus business and business education, to face and answer.

The twenty-first century business curriculum, therefore, will have to look at alternative sociopolitical and economic solutions. This will necessitate teaching different concepts and theories. Additional subjects, such as spirituality, languages, and in-depth cultural knowledge, already are emerging as important, and business educators soon may face the daunting task of acquiring different knowledge skills and rewriting much of what they have taught before.

Business educators must follow the same advice they give to corporations: look at waste, reduce it, prevent it, and redesign for a future that utilizes resources sustainably and shares knowledge responsibly. In the process they must be willing to give up established practices and academic sacred cows.

NOTE

1. Social Issues in Management (SIM) Division, Curriculum Development Committee (1990). *The Field of Business and Society: Ten Years after the Buchholz Study.* Symposium presented at the annual meeting of the Academy of Management, San Francisco.

REFERENCES

Carnegie Corporation. 1959. *Education of American Businessmen.* New York: Carnegie Corporation.

Collins, D., and S. L. Wartick. 1995. "Business and Society/Business Ethics Courses: Twenty Years at the Crossroads." *Business and Society* 34 (April): 51–89.

Dirksen, C. J., ed. 1966. *The American Assembly of Collegiate Schools of Business, 1916–1966.* Homewood, Ill.: Irwin.

Ford Foundation. 1959. *Higher Education for Business.* New York: Ford Foundation.

Gladwin, T. N. 1993. "The Meaning for Greening: A Plea for Organizational Theory." In *Environmental Strategies for Industry,* ed. K. Fischer and J. Schot, 37–61. Washington, D.C.: Island Press.

Gordon, R. A., and J. E. Howell. 1959. *Higher Education for Business.* New York: Columbia University Press.

Hart, Stuart L. 1997. "Beyond Greening: Strategies for a Sustainable World." *Harvard Business Review* (January-February): 66–76.

Kolluru, R. V., ed. 1994. *Environmental Strategies Handbook.* New York: McGraw-Hill.

Orr, D. 1995. "Greening of Education." *Resurgence* 170 (May–June): 16–19.

Whitmyer, C., ed. 1994. *Mindfulness and Meaningful Work: Explorations in Right Livelihood.* Berkeley, Calif.: Parallax Press.

THADDEUS C. TRZYNA

Sustainable Development

Linking Values and Policy

Described here is a new international program to build ethics into decision making to promote sustainable development. Doing so presents a double challenge, because I will need to explain two concepts—sustainable development and relating ethics to decision making—in a short space.

For a number of years I have been affiliated with the IUCN—the World Conservation Union, formally known as the International Union for Conservation of Nature and Natural Resources. IUCN is the umbrella organization of the world conservation movement. Founded in 1948, its headquarters are near Geneva. It is unique among international bodies in that its members are states, governmental agencies, and nongovernmental organizations—altogether about 850 members in 130 countries. IUCN cannot claim to have invented the concept of sustainable development, but it first gave the term wide currency when it issued the *World Conservation Strategy* in 1980 with the World Wide Fund for Nature and the United Nations Environment Programme (IUCN/UNEP/WWF 1980). Since then, IUCN has been involved in several dozen projects to formulate sustainable development strategies at national and local levels, and it has begun to synthesize this experience and that of others and try to make some sense out of it all.

75

Sustainable Development

Most people are familiar with the idea of sustainable development, which now occupies the center of thought on environmental and international development policy. It originated in the 1970s (Kidd 1992), began to be used in the international community with the publication of the *World Conservation Strategy,* and was popularized by the Brundtland Report, *Our Common Future* (WCED 1987), and *Agenda 21,* the document adopted by the 1992 United Nations Conference on Environment and Development in Rio de Janeiro (United Nations 1993).

IUCN defines sustainable development as "improving the quality of human life while living within the carrying capacity of supporting ecosystems." This comes from *Caring for the Earth: A Strategy for Sustainable Living,* the follow-up document to the *World Conservation Strategy* that IUCN produced with the same partners (IUCN/UNEP/WWF 1991).

Sustainable development is a misunderstood and often misused concept. In the United States, it is sometimes interpreted as trying to achieve a balance between environmental and economic interests in a simplistic way—trying to find a compromise somewhere in between. Or worse, it is distorted into something called "sustainable growth," whatever that might mean.

People with scientific or technical backgrounds often want a precise definition of sustainability and the means of measuring progress toward it. While it is useful to measure progress toward goals such as clean water, social equity, and public health, the point is often missed: The direction is more important than the precise goals or figures, and our energies are better spent on finding out what works to move us in that direction.

Sustainable development is many things. It is a social and political process, for example. It is also an integrating concept, a way of bringing together the ecological, economic, and social aspects of a problem, a holistic approach to things (Trzyna 1995).

But above all sustainable development is a moral principle. Improving the quality of life while living within the earth's carrying capacity is a moral principle. It is not so much about what is, but what should be. It has to do with value choices.

IUCN is an environmental organization, but in designing its ethics program we decided to focus not on environmental ethics but on ethics

applied to sustainable development, which is broader than—and sub-
sumes—environmental ethics. This is because ethics is really indivisible.
Environmental issues cannot be considered separately from economic and
social issues. Domestically and internationally, we cannot consider the
environment apart from such questions as equity, poverty, and human
rights.

In a discussion about moral choices, the head of environmental affairs
for a major international development agency described for me some of
the hard decisions that his organization has to make in allocating limited
funds for development assistance. A hypothetical example comes from a
country where I lived for two years, the Republic of Congo. Congo is a
large country, about the size of the United States east of the Mississippi
River, and immensely rich in natural resources. In terms of concentration
of biodiversity, it is one of the three leading countries in the world, along
with Brazil and Indonesia. Congo has been politically and economically
isolated for some time. What will happen when it opens up again to major aid and economic investment? Decisions need to be made on how to
allocate a limited amount of aid for a number of pressing needs, such as
protecting biodiversity while maintaining order, providing basic public
health services, repairing infrastructure, and shoring up governmental institutions. What will be the ethical basis of those decisions? Who will
make the moral choices?

Building Values into Decision Making

An examination of the rationale for IUCN's program is necessary to understand how it has evolved. IUCN has been wrestling with the
ethical dimensions of sustainable development for fifteen years. Since
1984 IUCN has had an active Ethics Working Group chaired by J. Ronald
Engel, professor of social ethics at the Meadville/Lombard Theological
School and the University of Chicago. We held workshops, produced some
excellent books (Engel and Engel 1990; Rockefeller and Elder 1992), and
contributed to a number of strategy documents.

But we in IUCN have been frustrated over where to go from there—
how to translate our ideas about ethics into policies, decisions, and practice. The usual way of answering this question is to talk about changing people's values through the educational system, religious groups, and

the media. And the metaphor often used is the one that describes turning around an oil tanker steaming full speed ahead—a difficult and long-term job.

The idea behind the IUCN program is that results are much more quickly realized by institutionalizing the process of taking ethics into account. In other words, making careful and systematic articulation of value choices an explicit part of policy formulation and decision making.

A New Program

The program will be conducted by a consortium that is in an early stage of organization. Among the participants already on board, in addition to IUCN, are the University of Michigan School of Natural Resources and Environment and six nongovernmental organizations on five continents: the Brazilian Foundation for Conservation of Nature; the California Institute of Public Affairs; Development Alternatives in New Delhi; the Environment Council in London; the Latin American Future Foundation in Quito, Ecuador; and the Zimbabwe National Environment Trust. Others will be joining us.

We plan to work cooperatively with several key organizations to build consideration of values into their decision-making processes. So far, we have had very productive discussions with the World Bank, the United States Agency for International Development, and the California legislature, among others.

Three Tools

In this new program, we plan to experiment with a number of tools for incorporating ethics into decision making, especially including ethics in policy analysis, including ethics in policy dialogues, and declaring principles. Here are some examples:

Including Ethics in Policy Analysis

Policy analysis is a method of looking at policy choices that has developed into a separate field of practice and study over the past thirty years. It includes environmental impact assessment and risk analysis. It is an attempt to bring scientific methods to bear on decision making, and it centers on one value: efficiency, or benefits in relation to cost. Policy analysis has deliberately steered clear of looking at what is right or wrong.

But an increasing number of writers on public policy are arguing that ethics should be included systematically in policy analysis (Amy 1984; Anderson 1979; Bergerson 1988; Dorfman 1976; Gillroy 1993; Linder 1986; Schelling 1981). Planners want to push this into practice, and hope to start with the environmental impact assessment process. One point of entry is the International Association for Impact Assessment, whose leaders are eager to work on this problem. Other points of entry, we hope, will be the World Bank and the U.S. federal and California state impact statement processes.

Including Ethics in Policy Dialogues

Policy dialogues, sometimes called roundtables or consensus groups, are increasingly popular ways of getting people who represent disparate interests to reach agreement on environmental issues (Trzyna and Gotelli 1989). Experience shows, however, that it is not enough to bring stakeholders around the table, even with a first-rate facilitator. Unless there is the vision of a common higher purpose, the discussions tend to stay at the level of searching for the lowest common denominator among the participants' special interests. Those interests reflect basic conflicts in values, and I believe ethics as a profession can help to clarify the value choices and move the discussion toward higher ground.

Political scientist Dale Jamieson (1992, 159) has written, "One of the most important benefits of viewing global environmental problems as moral problems is that this brings them into the domain of dialogue, discussion, and participation. Rather than being management problems that governments or experts can solve for us, when seen as ethical problems, they become problems for all of us to address, both as political actors and as everyday moral agents."

We hope to work on several fronts to bring ethics explicitly into policy dialogues. Three examples are under discussion: on wildlife issues in southern Africa, through IUCN and the Zimbabwe National Environment Trust; on biodiversity issues in California, through the California Institute of Public Affairs and the California State Senate; and on a range of sustainable development issues in the Western Hemisphere, with the Latin American Future Foundation and the Brazilian Foundation for Conservation of Nature.

Declaring Principles

Declarations of principles and codes of practice are important for two reasons: they set the tone for conduct and debate, and those who subscribe to these documents can then be held accountable to them, at least morally and politically, if not legally.

The IUCN group has worked on two broad global statements of principles: on the Earth Charter, with the Earth Council and others, and on the draft International Covenant on Environment and Development, with the IUCN Commission on Environmental Law.

The assumption behind all of this, the working hypothesis, is that if value choices are subjected to the same kind of rigorous analysis and discussion as facts, the people making decisions will be forced to consider the moral implications of those decisions. This is open to argument, of course, but there are some parallels in other fields (law and medicine, for instance), and those involved think it is worth trying.

Another basis of this approach is that people hold not a single value, of course, but complex sets of conflicting values, and if we make people ponder those values, we might get them to choose the high road.

In addition to what I have mentioned, an important part of this program will be surveying what is being done around the world to build ethics into decision making, looking at parallels in other fields, building a network, and synthesizing and disseminating results.

Five Issues

IUCN's policy ethics initiative was developed through a consultative process (funded by the Rockefeller Brothers Fund) that involved individual meetings and correspondence with well over a hundred people from many countries. We found strong support for the approach being taken, but a number of issues were raised frequently. Five of them in particular show the difficulty of linking ethics and decision making:

This will not be an easy task. Bringing ethics into decision making will not be easy to sell. This is the point made most often and most emphatically by those consulted about this initiative. For some people, "ethics" seems airy-fairy. To others, it sounds elitist. Still others are threatened by the value shifts that it implies. It cannot be emphasized too strongly that the program must be politically nonpartisan and conducted in a highly professional manner. How it will gain acceptance must receive serious attention.

Beware of sounding academic or moralistic. A related point, also often made, is that the program will fail if it has an academic style or moralistic tone. Scholars and spiritual leaders will be important to its success, but because it is directed at policymakers, its style must be the style of the policy arena. Among other things, this means being able to respond quickly to requests and opportunities; politicians and business executives have short time scales.

Whose ethics are we talking about? Will the program be biased toward a particular ethical stance? Certainly, it will be biased in the sense that sustainable development represents an ethical position or constellation of ethical principles. However, in practice, as Ralph Carter (1988, 287) points out, "Policy decisions usually involve tradeoffs between multiple values, and one option rarely emerges as clearly superior to others. Far from the ideal world of black and white options, the real world of political choice often seems a landscape distinguished only by the remarkable variation in shades of gray."

IUCN's contribution will be to clarify the ethical implications of those value choices. However, I must point out that the question of "whose ethics" is directly related to whether and how various stakeholders are represented in decision-making forums; analysis cannot be separated from process.

Is a universal ethic possible? The most difficult issue in dealing with ethics in an international context is the tension between unity and diversity. Ronald Engel (1994, 4–5) wrote, "For many, to speak of a global ethic smacks of a forced unity—something that will be imposed by one part of the world on other parts of the world, a new kind of colonialism. . . . On the other hand, there are many who are worried that we are drifting into a situation of 'cultural relativism'—whereby it is assumed that no one, except those who belong to a particular society, can or should say anything about the values of that society." Engel believes the answer is to recognize that there can be unity in variety, that it makes sense "to speak at one and the same time of 'a world ethic for living sustainably' and of 'world ethics for living sustainably.'" In other words, there should be global consensus on broad goals, but there can be a variety of ways of achieving them. Our program will be working at two levels: promoting sustainable development in a general way, and helping to resolve the ethical dilemmas that arise in trying to achieve it.

How do you find the people to do this? We need hybrids, people who relate to both policy and ethics, and they are not easy to find. There is probably a need for training here.

The Business Connection

The business element of our program will be centered at the Environment Council in London. The Council is a focal point for environmental groups in the United Kingdom and has a major business and environment program with some eight hundred business corporations as affiliates. Its relatively new Sustainable Business Forum will be the main locus for its ethics work with businesses. Our partner in India, Development Alternatives, also works with major corporations in innovative ways.

Much is being done to promote environmental protection and sustainable development in the business community, but we believe ethical analysis could be an important tool for getting companies to face value questions. Initial plans call for working closely with a small number of major transnational corporations.

Another avenue might be through the field of business ethics. This has become a large field of activity, with its own professional societies, consulting firms, journals, textbooks, conferences, and training courses. Business ethics typically deals with the rules of the business game, for example, keeping promises and being fair to the competition. However, there is a trend toward redefining business ethics to include the impact of a company's operations on the world at large. Some firms are now taking into account the "whole-life cost" of products, for example (Drummond and Bain 1994). Ethical assessments and similar mechanisms can help to ensure that proposals are measured against company or industry-wide statements of principles and codes of practice. The ultimate goal, of course, must be changing corporate culture.

Our initiative at IUCN has attracted a great deal of interest, but we are under no illusions that the task before us is an easy one.

REFERENCES

Amy, Douglas J. 1984. Why policy analysis and ethics are incompatible. *Journal of Policy Analysis and Management* 4:573–91.

Anderson, Charles W. 1979. The place of principles in policy analysis. *American Political Science Review* 73:711–23.

Bergerson, Peter J. 1988. *Ethics and Public Policy: An Annotated Bibliography.* New York: Garland.

Carter, Ralph G. 1988. Morality in the making of foreign policy. In *Ethics, Government, and Public Policy: A Reference Guide,* ed. James S. Bowman and Frederick A. Elliston, 287–305. Westport, Conn.: Greenwood Press.

Dorfman, Robert. 1976. An afterword: Humane values and environmental decisions. In *When Values Conflict,* ed. Lawrence Tribe, 153–73. Cambridge, Mass.: Ballinger.

Drummond, John, and Bill Bain, eds. 1994. *Managing Business Ethics.* Oxford: Butterworth-Heinemann.

Engel, J. Ronald. 1994. Our mandate for advancing a world ethic for living sustainably. Presented at a workshop on "A new ethics and a new covenant" at the IUCN General Assembly, Buenos Aires, January.

Engel, J. Ronald, and Joan Gibb Engel, eds. 1990. *Ethics of Environment and Development: Global Challenge, International Response.* London: Belhaven; Tucson: University of Arizona Press.

Gillroy, John Martin. 1993. *Environmental Risk, Environmental Values, and Political Choice: Beyond Efficiency Trade-offs in Public Policy Analysis.* Boulder, Colo.: Westview Press.

IUCN/UNEP/WWF. 1980. *World Conservation Strategy.* Gland, Switzerland: IUCN.

———. 1991. *Caring for the Earth: A Strategy for Sustainable Living.* Gland, Switzerland: IUCN.

Jamieson, Dale. 1992. Ethics, public policy, and global warming. *Science, Technology, and Human Values* 17:139–53.

Kidd, Charles V. 1992. The evolution of sustainability. *Journal of Agricultural and Environmental Ethics* 5(1): 1–26.

Linder, Stephen H. 1986. Efficiency, multiple claims, and moral values. In *Policy Analysis: Perspectives, Concepts, and Methods,* ed. William N. Dunn, 281–99. Greenwich, Conn.: JAI.

Rockefeller, Steven C., and John C. Elder, eds. 1992. *Spirit and Nature: Why the Environment Is a Religious Issue.* Boston: Beacon Press.

Schelling, Thomas C. 1981. Analytic methods and the ethics of policy. In *Ethics in Hard Times,* ed. Arthur L. Caplan and Daniel Callahan, 175–215. New York: Plenum.

Trzyna, Thaddeus C., ed. 1995. *A Sustainable World: Defining and Measuring Sustainable Development.* Sacramento: International Center for the Environment and Public Policy, California Institute of Public Affairs.

Trzyna, Thaddeus C., and Ilze M. Gotelli, eds. 1989. *The Power of Convening: Collaborative Policy Forums for Sustainable Development.* Claremont: California Institute of Public Affairs.

United Nations. 1993. *Agenda 21: Programme of Action for Sustainable Development.* New York: United Nations.

WCED. 1987. *Our Common Future: The Report of the World Commission on Environment and Development.* New York: Oxford University Press.

WARREN KRIESEL & TERENCE J. CENTNER

Environmental Justice

Establishing Evidence of Discrimination

Considerable evidence that minorities and the poor have experienced disproportionate exposure to various environmental hazards has been documented to advance claims of discrimination. One widely quoted book contains papers from the Conference on Race and the Incidence of Environmental Hazards held at the University of Michigan in 1990 (Bryant and Mohai 1992). Another work focuses on the American South, the region of residence to more than half of African Americans, to discuss environmental discrimination in the siting of noxious facilities (Bullard 1994). Various law reviews have drawn upon these works to create a commendable collection of materials on the issues of environmental racism and environmental justice. One of the most informative suggests that civil rights advocates should look to the environmental law framework in the pursuit of environmental justice (Foster 1993). Another commentary recommends an intermediate-level scrutiny test to address equal protection challenges based on environmental racism (Boyle 1993).

To address the public's concerns, the Office of Environmental Equity has been established within the EPA; it coordinates much of the work under its Environmental Justice Program. Further institutional action may be expected pursuant to President Clinton's Executive Order 12898 of February 1994. This order directed federal agencies to avoid inflicting disproportionate environmental harm on minorities and the poor, and a working group was established to "provide guidance to Federal agencies on criteria for identifying disproportionately high and adverse human health environmental effects on minority populations and low-income populations."

While the literature offers a wide range of supporting evidence that environmental problems exist for minorities and low-income populations, much of the evidence claiming to support or show racial discrimination consists of case studies or analyses that may lack sufficient empirical rigor to establish affirmatively evidence of discrimination based on race. This means that the evidence of many studies may not be sufficient to qualify a plaintiff for relief under existing constitutional and statutory courses of action. For example, in a recent challenge to the discriminatory siting of a regional landfill based on an equal protection argument, the court found insufficient evidence to show intentional racial discrimination (*RISE, Inc. v Kay* 1991). Instead, the district court suggested that the siting was due to economic and legal conditions and "the relative environmental suitability of the sites."

Many of the existing studies also do not differentiate between the effect of income as opposed to race. The economics of the housing market suggest that environmentally undesirable localities are more likely to be populated by low-income people. While society may want to fashion responses to such environmental injustice, most existing institutional remedies for environmental racism must be founded on discrimination that is based solely on race and not income. An exception to this is Title VI of the Civil Rights Act of 1964, which prohibits discrimination based on race, color, or national origin from any program or activity receiving federal financial assistance. Actions can be initiated under Title VI regardless of the discriminated party's income status, but the scope of such actions is limited by the requirement that the discrimination has resulted from a program that has received federal funds.

Difficulties involving the use of statistical methods that can conclusively show environmental discrimination based on race raise a question of how to achieve the more equitable treatment of all persons (Centner, Kriesel, and Keeler 1996). Individual laws regulating the siting of undesirable facilities might incorporate more specific public notice requirements (Saleem 1994). Citizen suit provisions of major federal legislation might be more vigorously employed to seek redress (Guana 1995). Another recommendation is to place greater reliance on private compensation, including preventive compensation to ameliorate adverse effects, remedial compensation for damages suffered, or incentive payments to the host community (Mank 1995). By applying one or all of these suggestions, injustices involving the location of environmental dangers might be tempered to achieve a more noble resolution of conflicting interests.

This chapter contains two analyses of whether environmental inequity exists. Both analyses use geographic information system–related data to construct a dependent variable that represents the area-weighted poundage of released toxic materials for 7,292 Census block groups in Georgia. We separately tested for whether minority or poor neighborhoods have disproportionate exposure to environmental risks, and whether these neighborhoods have been targeted to host toxic facilities.

Differential Exposure and Racial Discrimination

Three collections of literature offer insight to the issue of whether poor or minority neighborhoods may be exposed to higher environmental risks. First, the literature in the economics of urban amenities suggests that higher-income households will locate in areas with higher-quality environmental amenities (Diamond and Tolley 1982). Within a region, households will select housing locations according to their preferences for local public goods and services, including environmental amenities, subject to their budget constraints. To the extent that environmental quality is purchased in the housing market, higher-income households tend to sort themselves out into neighborhoods with higher environmental quality. This housing market process is dynamic: neighborhood adjustments are made whenever a household makes an ordinary relocation or a neighborhood has experienced a change in environmental amenities. As a result, the price of high-quality locations will be bid up, and poor households are left with affordable housing located in relatively polluted areas. The literature provides no explicit consideration of how race might matter in pollution exposure. To the extent that minority groups may be poor, it may be inferred that such persons will be exposed to higher ambient pollution levels.

The environmental justice literature contains analyses and studies that

report minorities and low-income groups being disproportionately subjected to pollutants and environmental risks. For example, the reports by
Bryant and Mohai summarize fifteen studies that examine the burden of
environmental risk by income and/or racial groups. After reviewing the
factors that led to the observed distribution of pollution, including disadvantages in the availability of resources and underrepresentation on gov-
erning bodies, Bryant and Mohai (1992, 160) conclude, "Taken together,
these factors suggest that race has an additional impact on the distribution of environmental hazards, independent of income."

Such a conclusion, however, is not clear when the rigor of the empirical tests is evaluated. Of the fifteen studies, Bryant and Mohai state that
nine are amenable to a comparison of the relative importance of race
or income in determining an area's pollutant concentration. The typical
study compares the correlation coefficients for an area's income and racial characteristics with pollutant levels to show that race was the best
predictor of where environmental risks occurred. However, correlation
analysis by itself is not capable of controlling for the effect that income
plays in determining a racial group's exposure. Multiple regression is a
better technique.

The association between environmental quality and a locality's racial
and income characteristics has been recognized in the environmental economics literature that examines the distribution of air quality and benefits. In an early study, Zubin (1973) found a negative correlation coefficient between pollution levels and income. Negative correlations for
income and race were found by Harrison and Rubinfeld (1978) and Asch
and Seneca (1978). More recent research focuses on an individual's total
exposure to air pollutants, which includes conditions not only at the place
of residence but also at the place of work, school, and recreation (Brajer
and Hall 1992). None of these studies employed a technique capable of
separating income's effect from race.

Tobit Analysis of Toxic Releases

To test whether neighborhoods with predominantly nonwhite or
poor residents may be exposed to higher environmental hazards, we employed data from the 1990 Census of population. A neighborhood is

defined as a Census block group (of which there are 7,292 in Georgia). In this analysis, each neighborhood is assigned its racial characteristic, defined as the percentage of nonwhite population; its income characteristic, defined as the percentage of population living in poverty; and a dummy variable that was one if the block group was in a metropolitan area and that was zero otherwise. There are other income measures (for example, per capita income), but the percentage of population in poverty is preferred because it has been used in other studies of environmental justice, and it is in the same percentage terms as the racial variable. Moreover, Census block groups are sufficiently small units of observation that should come close to approximating the neighborhood effects that the environmental justice literature argues is most crucial.

Our measure of exposure to environmental risk is from the EPA's toxic release inventory (TRI) data set. The TRI data summarize annual reports filed by firms, as mandated under Section 313 of the Emergency Planning and Community Right-to-Know Act of the Superfund Amendments and Reauthorization Act of 1986. To perform the analysis we calculated the annual average poundage of released toxics reported by 884 establishments in Georgia from 1987 to 1992.

The location of each Census block group is identified on the CD-ROM by the latitude and longitude (to within 0.000001 of a degree) of its centroid. The area, convertible to square miles, is also reported for each block group. With these data it was possible to define each block group's north, south, east, and west boundaries with a simple SAS routine and the assumption that block groups tend to be square. Similarly, the TRI data report the latitude and longitude of each establishment. Assuming that the impact of toxic materials is limited to within one mile of a TRI site we were able to calculate, for each block group, the area of the union of a block group and each TRI establishment. The block group was assigned the poundage of toxic materials from the TRI site, based on the proportion of the union's area to the one-mile toxic area. This process was repeated for each TRI establishment within one mile of a block group's boundaries, and the poundages were summed to yield the annual average poundage of toxic material to which a Census block group potentially is exposed.

The summary statistics are as follows. For the 7,292 block groups,

4,409 were farther than one mile from a TRI site and they were not exposed to toxic releases as defined here. The average exposure for the remaining 2,883 block groups was 252,198 pounds per year. The average nonwhite population was 27.76 percent, the average percentage of population in poverty was 16.47, and the percentage of neighborhoods located in metropolitan areas was 56.85 percent. The correlation between nonwhite population and poverty was 0.544. This relatively low correlation between race and poverty highlights the advantage of conducting this analysis in a state such as Georgia. Multicollinearity is not a problem because there are majority white poor areas as well as majority black poor areas in rural, suburban, and metropolitan environs.

Our dependent variable is obviously censored at zero. Ordinary least squares regression would yield biased and inefficient estimators because the method cannot account for nonzero means of the disturbance term that the censoring causes (Greene 1993). In this situation tobit regression should be applied.

The results are presented in table 1, with model 1 representing the full set of 7,292 observations. A pretest indicated a need for applying the log transformation to the dependent variable, while the independent variables remain linear. The racial, poverty, and metropolitan variables are positive, as hypothesized, and the one-tailed test for all variables is rejected at the 0.05 significance level. The coefficient for the 0–1 dummy variable can be interpreted as saying that toxic releases in metropolitan block groups average 10.26 pounds (the antilog of 2.3) more than nonmetropolitan block groups. Thus, between cities and rural areas there is a very small difference in toxic releases.

Concerning whether race or poverty characteristics matter more, both of our variables are in percentage terms so that a direct comparison of the coefficients can be made. In particular, with this type of semilog functional form, the racial coefficient of 4.9 can be interpreted as saying that a 1 percent increase in a block group's nonwhite population will lead to a 4.9 percent increase in toxic substance release (because the independent variable is in percentage terms). Similarly, the poverty coefficient indicates that a 1 percent increase in a block group's population in poverty will lead to a 5.3 percent increase in the release of toxic substances. These values are quite close, but the racial variable's standard error is half of poverty's,

Table 1. Tobit Regression Analysis of Toxic Release Data

	"Exposure to Ambient Risks" Model		"Targeting" Model
	Model 1 All Observations	Model 2 Random Sample	Model 3
Percentage of nonwhite population	4.968	10.728	1.951
	(0.481)*	(4.151)*	(1.547)
Percentage of population in poverty	5.353	8.889	0.265
	(0.894)*	(7.484)	(2.919)
0-1 Variable, Census block group located in metropolitan area	2.329	0.134	−0.912
	(0.274)*	(2.534)	(0.868)
Intercept	−5.293	−8.254	−28.245
	(0.286)*	(2.694)*	(1.779)*
N	7,292	100	7,292
Number of left-censored observations	4,409	66	7,000

Note: The dependent variable is the log of the area-weighted average annual pounds of toxic material released between 1987 and 1992 in a Census block group area. Standard errors of parameter estimates are in parentheses.

* Significant at $p < 0.05$.

so we conclude that while poverty's effect is slightly greater than race's, the racial effect is more certain.

As further evidence, we note that among those block groups within one mile of a TRI site the average percentage of nonwhite population is 35.2 percent, higher than the 22.9 percent average for the 4,409 block groups located farther away from the TRI sites. A comparison for the other variable is 19.45 percent living in poverty for block groups within one mile of a TRI site versus 14.5 percent for those farther away. Thus, we conclude that a block group's racial and poverty characteristics influence exposure to toxic materials.

From model 1's results in table 1 a conclusion can be reached: that both race and poverty matter in determining a block group's level of exposure to environmental hazards. However, one wonders whether the 7,292 block groups represent a random sample or the universe of all Georgia areas. When there is a possibility that the latter condition exists, then Leamer's (1978) criticism should be noted: that the large number of observations has reduced the power of the hypothesis tests, and the likelihood of committing a type 1 error is increased.

According to Leamer there are two ways to reduce the probability of a type 1 error. One is to decrease the significance level. If $\alpha = 0.01$ is used instead of 0.05, then our current results remain unchanged. Another approach is to reduce the size of the data set by taking a random sample. A random sampling routine was written to yield a subsample, with the number of observations arbitrarily limited at $N = 100$. This process was repeated forty times, with tobit analyses performed on each, so that we could gain additional insights.

Of these forty subsamples, the racial variable had a positive, significant influence in eighteen models, poverty had the same effect in ten models, and the dummy variable had the effect in eight models. Model 2 in table 1 reports the results from a typical model. Here, the race variable has a significant, positive effect, whereas poverty's effect is smaller and insignificant. We feel confident with these results because they are derived from a more powerful test than that used in model 1, and we conclude that both race and poverty matter in determining environmental risks, although poverty's effect is less certain.

Minority Areas Targeted to Host Undesirable Land Uses

As in the debate over differential exposure, the targeting debate has produced an impressive body of literature. A 1982 landfill protest campaign in North Carolina prompted a General Accounting Office report which found that three out of every four commercial hazardous waste landfills in the southeastern United States were located in majority black communities. In 1987, the United Church of Christ Commission for Racial Justice analyzed the relationship between race and location of hazard sites. The commission found race to be the predominant factor related to the siting of hazardous wastes in communities throughout the United States.

According to a 1987 study, more than 15 million of the nation's 26 million blacks and over 8 million of the 15 million Hispanics live in communities with one or more toxic waste sites (Commission for Racial Justice 1987). In addition, three of the U.S. major hazardous waste landfills are located in areas where the population is predominantly black or Hispanic. A 1992 study claimed that a result of the not-in-my-backyard (NIMBY) syndrome is that such facilities will tend to be located in communities with the least ability to mount a protest (Environmental Equity Workgroup 1992).

In his 1994 book, *Dumping in Dixie,* Bullard cites newspaper articles and his own personal interviews in minority communities that host waste facilities, chemical plants, petroleum refineries, etc. He states that facility location results from planners' conscious targeting of minority communities. Bullard attributes the planners' motivation to the fact that minority communities lack the ability to fight the decision process, which is due in turn to a lack of monetary resources that could purchase high-quality legal counsel and the lack of representation in the political process. While this explanation has intuitive appeal, similar conditions may exist in poor white communities so that the special influence of race in the decision process would be nullified.

We find two shortcomings with the research methods employed in previous studies. First, a finding that polluting industries are grouped around minority neighborhoods does not prove that targeting has occurred. The finding may be explained by housing market dynamics that could result in poor people locating in neighborhoods subsequent to the noxious industry location (and after property values have declined). An empirical analysis to test targeting should focus on recently located facilities and the local racial and poverty characteristics at the time that location decisions were made.

The second shortcoming is the reliance on the case study research method. In a case study, the investigator employs personal interviews and information from various sources to explain what caused a "locally unwanted land use" (LULU) to be located in a particular site. However, the case study method is only one of many research tools that the investigator can employ in understanding the role that community characteristics, including race, play in LULU location. Our method, which we argue is more objective, analyzes toxic facility location patterns for 7,292 observations within a multiple regression context.

Tobit Analysis of Recently Located TRI Sites

To discern whether there is environmental inequity with respect to firms' targeting of minority and poor neighborhoods, our empirical test focuses on the location patterns of TRI sites that have been established close to the time of the 1990 Census. This analysis is similar to that in the previous section; that is, we sum the area-weighted poundages of toxic materials released within one mile of each of the 7,292 Census block groups in Georgia. However, here we sum only the toxics emitted by firms that have located between 1987 and 1992. This analysis was made possible by matching the TRI firm's name and location with a listing of new manufacturing plants compiled by the Georgia Department of Industry, Trade, and Tourism.

Of the 884 TRI facilities, only seventy-one had located between 1987 and 1992. Nonetheless, these seventy-one sites are within one mile of 292 block groups, so that 4 percent of the 7,292 block groups are not censored at zero. The summary statistics for variables in the location model are identical to those reported in the previous section, except that the average annual poundage of released toxics from recently located TRI sites is 37,461 pounds. If the firms' managers targeted poor and/or minority neighborhoods to host their facilities, then a tobit regression should yield positive coefficients for the racial and poverty variables. Indeed, the results reported for model 3 in table 1 indicate that both race and poverty have a positive influence on a block group's exposure to toxic materials, but the effects are not statistically different from zero. As further evidence, we note that among those block groups within one mile of a TRI site the average percentage of nonwhite population is 30.3 percent (for poverty it is 17.3 percent), slightly higher than the 27.7 percent average (for poverty, 16.4 percent) for the 7,000 block groups located farther away from the TRI sites. Thus, we conclude that targeting of noxious facilities has not occurred within the period we examine. Rather, recent industrial location research for the state of Georgia has found that public services, labor market conditions, and location incentives were important predictors of plant location (Kriesel and McNamara 1991).

Conclusions

This issue of environmental equity has come about slowly since the 1970s and is gaining increased visibility in both environmental and civil rights circles. This is due to the growth of information about the relationship between environmental hazards and health, especially among minority and low-income populations. The studies showing the relationship between race, poverty, and environmental conditions have indicated that hazardous facilities and polluting industries may be disproportionately located in minority neighborhoods. Court cases alleging violation of the Fourteenth Amendment's Equal Protection Clause subsequently have failed to find any evidence of intent to discriminate.

From this empirical analysis of the toxic release inventory data for the state of Georgia, we conclude that race and poverty both matter in determining burdens of released toxic materials. The targeting analysis indicates that neither race nor income is important in determining whether minority and poor communities have been targeted to host facilities that are on the TRI list. This result can be attributed to the more important role that other traditional location factors, such as the presence of agglomeration economies, labor market characteristics, etc., play in the location decisions made by firms. Thus, a speculation can be made: that if firms' location behavior has not changed over the years, then the results suggest that housing market dynamics are the main reason why the poor are exposed to higher environmental risks. However, we are at a loss to explain why nonwhites are exposed to higher risks even after accounting for their income levels. Probably this is due to the same frictions in the housing market that have produced persistently segregated neighborhoods. As such, disproportionate risk burdens by racial minorities are another product of the poor state of American racial equality.

The results suggest two additional conclusions that are cause for societal concern. First, the finding that a neighborhood's poverty characteristics are associated with higher environmental risks is a violation of vertical equity, that is, the equal treatment of people with dissimilar incomes. Regarding access to ordinary marketed goods such as food and housing, most capitalist societies tolerate vertical inequity. Within a market economy, the individual is expected to view the prospect of vertical inequity as an incentive to work harder in order to obtain the income needed to overcome this inequity. Of course, some societies employ safety net policies that ensure a minimal standard of living. Within the United States, these policies have addressed not only income maintenance but also housing, education, and health. The question of whether American society wishes to add environmental protection to the list of safety net guarantees is an important one that underlies the current debate about environmental justice.

Second, the finding that a neighborhood's racial characteristics are associated with higher environmental risks is a violation of horizontal equity, that is, the equal treatment of people with similar incomes. Again, this finding comes from table 1: If the poverty effect were totally responsible for determining environmental risk burdens (as economic theory suggests), then the racial variable would not have been statistically significant. Our finding that it is significant implies that nonwhites are subjected to higher environmental risks, even after accounting for their income level. American society has generally not accepted horizontal inequity because it is opposed to the high value that western political philosophy has placed on the equality of individuals (Samuelson and Nordhaus 1994). If environmental activists wish to pursue legislative relief for victims of environmental injustice as suggested by Foster (1993), the evidence from Georgia strongly supports arguments based on the violation of horizontal equity.

REFERENCES

Asch, P., and J. J. Seneca. 1978. "Some Evidence on the Distribution of Air Quality." *Land Economics* 55:278–97.

Boyle, E. P. 1993. "It's Not Easy Being Green: The Psychology of Racism, Environmental Discrimination, and the Argument for Modernizing Equal Protection Analysis." *Vanderbilt Law Review* 46:937–89.

Brajer, V., and J. V. Hall. 1992. "Recent Evidence on the Distribution of Air Pollution Effects." *Contemporary Policy Issues* 6:63–71.

Bryant, B., and P. Mohai. 1992. *Race and the Incidence of Environmental Hazards: A Time for Discourse*. Boulder: Westview Press.

Bullard, R. D. 1994. *Dumping in Dixie: Race, Class, and Environmental Quality.* 2d ed. San Francisco: Westview Press.

Centner, T. J., W. Kriesel, and A. G. Keeler. 1996. "Environmental Justice and Toxic Releases: Establishing Evidence of Discriminatory Effect Based on Race and Not Income." *Wisconsin Environmental Law Journal* 3:119–58.

Commission for Racial Justice, United Church of Christ. 1987. *Toxic Wastes and Race in the United States: A National Report on the Racial and Socioeconomic Characteristics of Communities with Hazardous Waste Sites,* xiii.

Diamond, D. B., and G. S. Tolley. 1982. *The Economics of Urban Amenities.* Orlando: Academic Press.

Environmental Equity Workgroup, U.S. Environmental Protection Agency. 1992. *Environmental Equity: Reducing Risk for All Communities,* 1:20–21.

Foster, S. 1993. "Racial Matters: The Quest for Environmental Justice." *Ecology Law Quarterly* 20:721–54.

Greene, W. H. 1993. *Econometric Analysis.* 2d ed. New York: Macmillan.

Guana, E. 1995. "Federal Environmental Citizen Provisions: Obstacles and Incentives on the Road to Environmental Justice." *Ecology Law Quarterly* 22:1–87.

Harrison, D. Jr., and Daniel Rubinfeld. 1978. "The Distribution of Benefits from Improvements in Urban Air Quality." *Journal of Environmental Economics and Management* 6:313–32.

Kriesel, W., and K. McNamara. 1991. "A County-Level Model of Manufacturing Plant Recruitment with Improved Industrial Site Quality Measurement." *Southern Journal of Agricultural Economics* 23(1):121–28.

Leamer, E. 1978. *Specification Searches: Ad Hoc Inferences with Nonexperimental Data.* New York: Wiley.

Mank, B. C. 1995. "Environmental Justice and Discriminatory Siting: Risk-Based Representation and Equitable Compensation." *Ohio State Law Journal* 56: 329–425.

RISE, Inc. v Kay, 768 F. Supp. 1144 (E.D. Vir. 1991), aff'd Case No. 91–2142 (4th Cir. 1992).

Saleem, O. 1994. "Overcoming Environmental Discrimination: The Need for a Disparate Impact Test and Improved Notice Requirements in Facility Siting Decisions." *Columbia Journal of Environmental Law* 19:211–49.

Samuelson, P. A., and William D. Nordhaus. 1994. *Economics.* 15th ed. New York: McGraw-Hill.

Zubin, J. M. 1973. *The Distribution of Air Quality in the New York Region.* Baltimore: Johns Hopkins University Press.

WILLIAM J. MCKINNEY

On the Value of Thought Experiments in the Industrial Marketplace

Science and technology cannot foresee every possible consequence of human actions in the environment. This "problem of prediction" has both epistemological and ethical dimensions. Hans Jonas (1984) argues convincingly that an "imperative of responsibility" in environmental and technological ethics emerges from the problem of prediction. Holmes Rolston (1988) has carried this line one step further, maintaining that we should refrain from actions in the environment for which we lack adequate information about potentially harmful consequences. Such is Rolston's gloss on the precautionary principle, which he uses to set limits on permissible corporate actions, arguing that corporations act ethically only if they assume that their actions are potentially harmful, and then strive to demonstrate otherwise before implementing that action. Yet a simple query presents itself: how can environmentally responsible scientific and market decisions be made in the absence of reliable information about the environment and the consequences of our actions therein?

On Predicting Technological Consequences

It is strangely ironic that while technology often strives to benefit the greatest number of people with the consequences of its actions, it is limited in its power to evaluate those very consequences accurately.[1] Confirmation theory in science recognizes that unforeseen experimental results are often an indication of faulty instrumentation, incomplete or inaccurate theories, or the locus of new discovery. Engineers recognize unforeseen consequences in the margins of error that they allow in their designs. However, when these uncertainties pose threats to human health and endanger the very environment upon which all living things depend for their survival, the ethical question of unforeseen consequences must be addressed. J. Ellul (1972, 103–4) has referred to this as the ambiguity of technical progress: "When scientists carry out their researches in one or another discipline and hit upon new technical means, they generally see clearly in what sphere the new technology will be applicable. Certain results are expected and gotten. *But,* there are always secondary effects which had not been anticipated, which in the primary stage of technological progress could not *in principle* have been anticipated. This unpredictability arises from the fact that predictability implies complete possibility of experimenting in *every* sphere, an inconceivable state of affairs."

What makes predictability useful in science is not the ability to test every prediction now but the ability to test predictions in principle. However, the fact that every possible outcome of a technological implementation cannot be known does remain problematic. In addition, and perhaps more troubling, is the fact that probabilistic predictions remain just that, probability assessments, and as such are prone to the uncertainties associated with all games of chance.[2] How can businesspersons and policymakers use scientific evidence and technological means to make ethically responsible environmental decisions?

Jonas and the Imperative of Responsibility

Given the uncertainty inherent in probability assessments and the ambiguity of technical progress, business and industry face the very real problem of a fundamental dichotomy between their power to act in the environment and their ability to predict the consequences of those actions through science and technology. This epistemic conclusion is ultimately problematic in an ethical sense. Jonas's imperative of responsibility extends from the dichotomy between our available knowledge of the natural world and humankind's ability to act upon that knowledge through science and technology. "*Knowledge,* under these circumstances, becomes a prime duty beyond anything for it heretofore, and the knowledge must be commensurate with the causal scale of our action. The fact that it cannot really be thus commensurate, that is, that the predictive knowledge falls behind the technical knowledge that nourishes our power to act, itself assumes ethical importance. The gap between the ability to foretell and the power to act creates a novel moral problem" (Jonas 1984, 7–8).

It is largely this discrepancy between our ability to predict and our ability to act which leads Jonas to develop a new ethic for technology and its relation to the environment. Yet the issue goes much deeper than this, for it could be argued that technology has always existed in a state where our ability to predict the consequences of its application falls behind our capacity to apply it. In fact, it was not until the nineteenth century that the predictive force of Newtonian mathematical science was used in a large-scale technological context.[3] As a result, modern technology is, if anything, capable of *greater* predictive powers than premodern, artisan-based technologies.

So, the real issue for Jonas is the scope of modern technology rather than its essential nature. According to Jonas, modern technology has the ability to harm nature beyond its capacities for self-repair. Modern technology is distinguished not in kind but in the scope of its cumulative and often irreversible effects. If this is indeed the case, then these unforeseen consequences may even supersede the knowledge upon which the original action was based, leaving us with little or no means of remedying detrimental situations (for example, the explosion at Chernobyl). Such is the basis of Jonas's "imperative of responsibility"—that is, that technological consequences have a moral component. Jonas argues that in the face of potential disasters whose solutions lie beyond the capacity of our knowledge base, we must recognize a nonreciprocal responsibility to future generations, analogous to the responsibility of parents toward their children. "Here is the archetype of all responsible action, which fortunately requires no deduction from a principle, because it is powerfully implanted in us by nature" (Jonas 1984, 39). Jonas argues from this basis for an environmental ethic that links human interests inextricably with those of the environment as a whole.

Given this basis for responsibility, how are we to act? The problem remains that our technology often has unforeseen consequences. It seems that, in addition to the imperative of responsibility, we need a guide for acting responsibly in light of our imperfect knowledge of technological consequences and the potentially devastating scope of those consequences.

Jonas offers such guidance in the form of a return to Aristotelian, as opposed to Baconian, science. He characterizes Aristotelian science as contemplative and Baconian as interventionistic: "Any 'Aristotelian' idea of a safe teleology of 'Nature' (*physis*) as a whole that attends to itself and automatically ensures the harmonizing of the many purposes into one is refuted by this latest turn. . . . To him, it was theoretical reason in man which stood out above nature and which surely did it no harm in contemplating it. . . . As long as practical intelligence and theoretical intellect went their separate ways, his [humankind's] impact on the balance of things remained tolerable" (Jonas 1984, 138).

Jonas contrasts this attitude with that of the Baconian ideal that knowledge about nature is power to control nature or, more accurately, to manipulate and intervene in nature. This conjunction of power and reason carries with it the imperative of responsibility. According to Jonas, responsibility demands that we act in accordance with our contemplative faculty before we exercise our ability to intervene in nature.

This reemphasis on the contemplative faculty stresses the role of thought experiments in industrial decision making. Thought experiments allow the engineer to extrapolate from present actions to the possibility of future ecological disasters before that harm occurs. Jonas argues that this is an ethical extrapolation which science and technology cannot give us. Thus, the imperative of responsibility rests on the power of the imagination to conceive of the detrimental effects of technological action, much like the imaginations of Orwell and Huxley have warned of future political and social problems (Jonas 1984, 30). "The perceived possibility can now take the place of the actual occasion; and reflection on the possible, fully unfolded in the imagination, gives access to new moral truth" (29). The power of imagination is to be used as a heuristic, a map from the realm of ideas which points to possible sources of ecological destruction in the external world. Jonas characterizes this heuristic as a "heuristic of fear," arguing that imagined ecological disasters are easier to prevent than actual disasters are to remedy. "That is the case with the 'ethics of the future' which we are looking for, where that which is to be feared has never yet happened and has perhaps no analogies in past or present experience. Then the creatively imagined *malum* has to take over the role of the experienced *malum*" (27).

This is the point at which I begin to disagree with Jonas. He has introduced the imperative of technological responsibility for all the right reasons (Rolston 1988, 319). My question is not whether we should use thought experiments; we should and indeed do. However, Jonas's prescription rests on a misunderstanding of both thought experiments and the Aristotelian natural philosophy to which he longs to return. As I argue here, thought experiments cannot occur *in vacuo*. Thought experiments draw their inspiration from present problems and background knowledge regarding the physical world, and thus, contrary to the passage cited above, do have analogues in past and/or present experience.

What Thought Experiments Can Do and What They Cannot Do

Thought experiments have played an important role in the history of science. One need only look to Mach's discussions of the power of the *Gedankenexperimente,* Galileo's neo-Pythagorean musings on pendula, and Einstein's fabled ride on a beam of light to realize the role they play in scientific discovery. Jonas wishes, however, for thought experiments to play a more active role—that of giving us new knowledge about the world. Care must be taken here. Thought experiments are an excellent tool for the formulation and clarification of concepts, but we must remember that thought experiments actually depend on "external world" experiments and are thus no substitute for them.

What Thought Experiments Can Do

Thought experiments are exercises in Neoplatonic science and are the work of rationalism par excellence. In thought experiments, science is revealed as a part of philosophy, not an institution distinct from it.[4] In thought experiments, the scientist can transcend many of the problems that beset external world experiments. It is only in thought that we can have frictionless pulleys and inclined planes, weightless ropes, and earth-bound falling bodies which are dropped at the same instant while suffering no air resistance (as in Galileo's experiments at Pisa). It is only in thought that such abstraction to the ideal is possible.

In this sense, thought experiment plays an essential role in science. The manifold of our experience presents the investigator or inventor with far too many parameters to either consider or manipulate at any one time. In addition, for any one phenomenon, there are an infinite number of logically possible explanations; for any one technological act, there are an infinite number of logically possible consequences. Thought experiments allow us to narrow these infinite search spaces, thus permitting the consideration of more workable, finite spaces of plausible hypotheses and feasible consequences. Yet we must remember that thought experiments are conducted in a number of possible worlds, none of which may be the physical world. While this may be fine for the natural philosopher such as Galileo, whose thought experiments in kinematics allowed the conception of inertial motion, it is clearly insufficient for the engineer whose design for a chemical plant has the ability to pollute real air and real water, harming real living things in the physical world.

Such a discrepancy in the utility of thought experiments points to the question of the link between the idealized worlds of thought experiments and the physical world which we seek to explain, to control, and to predict. In short, how are we to glean plausibility and feasibility from the infinite space of logical possibility? Mach (1984) argued that thought experiments reveal innate knowledge, allowing the thought experimenter to reflect what is going on in the external world by experiencing the reflections of those empirical realities in his/her thoughts. Yet pure thought alone will not give us knowledge about the world in which we live. In order to derive full benefit from thought experiments, there must be some form of empirical base from which to draw the plausibility and feasibility criteria so necessary in thought experiments. Consequently, Mach also drew on a sensationalist epistemology, where thought experiments were actually reflections of both innate knowledge and the evidence of sense data. This empirical experience cannot be undervalued, for it provides the background against which the set of all possible worlds is reduced to a more manageable set of feasible or plausible worlds. In short, this set of feasible worlds becomes plausible precisely because of analogy to past experiences (Hanson 1958).

What Thought Experiments Cannot Do

What is the link between the physical world and thought experiments, and in what sense are thought experiments really experiments? There are certain points of similarity between thought experiments and their external world counterparts. After all, both attempt the manipulation of certain parameters in order to bring forth some expected result. Yet consider the following which Sorensen (1992, 230) refers to as "points of resemblance" between thought and empirical experiments: failures of naive inductivism and tinkering. While both thought and empirical experiments are subject to the pitfalls of naive inductivism, inductive reasoning is, of course, applied to the interpretation of experimental data, rather than the design or the execution of experiments, thought or otherwise. Naive inductivism is naive because of the expectation that the physical world will behave in the future as it has in the past.

In an admittedly naive fashion, we can construct scientific inference as:

H_{mr} = df the hypothesis that the action in the environment entails minimal risk, and
p = df a prediction of a consequence of H_{mr}
where a positive realization of p *supports* H_{mr}.

Such is the stereotypical hypothetico-deductive (H-D) method. Unfortunately, as Glymour (1980) shows, H-D inferences are hopeless. His elegant proof can be paraphrased as follows.

Since H_{mr} alone cannot predict p, it must be conjoined with a broader set of assumptions and theoretical commitments (call it A). Glymour proves that, in virtue of this conjunction, H_{mr} is confirmed in the context of A, and p confirms H_{mr} only if p deductively entails H_{mr}. That is to say, given the truth of the positive test result, the hypothesis must also be true. This is problematic for, as we know, no single piece of evidence can deductively entail a hypothesis of universal form. In addition, if p really does deductively entail H_{mr}, then H_{mr} has no predictive import, for if it is entailed by p, it has only as much information content as p itself and can yield no additional predictions beyond the content of p.

What does this mean for our purposes? Apart from illustrating that the H-D model is hopeless, it demonstrates its dependence on the set A. While

Glymour stipulates that A not entail p in order to avoid ad hoc predictions, it is the case then that H_{mr} must entail p, for (H_{mr} and A) entail p. Since he proves that p does itself entail H_{mr}, then the prediction is vacuous, and its positive realization in experiment should give us no more confidence in H_{mr} than before experimental testing. The dilemma for our purposes is thus:

1. Prediction of p is at least partially contingent upon selection of A; or
2. H_{mr} has no predictive force at all, and thus we can have no evidential reason for justifiably believing it.

Our choice, then, is between a realization that the evidence alone cannot support a hypothesis and the fact that our hypotheses offer us no basis for predicting the consequences of our actions. It would seem as if we must accept 1 while rejecting 2. Yet this leaves us with the unwieldy "credit problem."[5]

If our justified belief in a hypothesis is to be based on the realization of its predictions, and those predictions are in part derived from a set of auxiliary assumptions, how are we to be certain that it is the hypothesis, and not the auxiliary assumptions, which we are confirming? There is no way of knowing whether or not p merely supports H_{mr}, merely supports A, or lends support to them both. In any case, if it is not the former, then it is possible that we are no farther along in believing that our environmental action carries minimal risk or whether our test result occurred as a consequence of experimental design, faulty instrumentation, human error, or another possible problem. The credit problem thus infects any choice to believe a hypothesis based on positive evidence, and whether we deem an action "innocent until proven guilty," or "guilty until proven innocent," the problems are logically identical. If we act presuming innocence, that presumption was made with some sort of inductive inference in some epistemological matrix. Given a faulty set A, we might assess that H_{mr} is justifiably believable, and err due not to H_{mr} itself but to our assumptions in A. Yet, since thought experiments can be as ideal as the thought experimenter desires them to be, there is no interaction between the experiment and the external world, which will behave on its own regardless of human preconceptions in set A.

Experimenters in the physical world do not have such luxury. There is an important difference between thought experiments and their empirical relatives, and that difference rests precisely in their design and execution in the physical world. Physical experiments do not always work because they must interact in a world that need not cooperate with our theories and expectations. So, in this sense, the problems of naive induction reveal a dissimilarity rather than a similarity. These are precisely the problems in the design and execution of empirical experiments that help the scientists conducting them to learn about the world in which they are intervening. Hacking (1983) was indeed correct when he maintained that "experiments don't always work." Precisely because they don't always work, scientists must tinker with their apparatus in order to gather desired results. Yet, by "tinkering," Sorensen does not mean tinkering in the sense of the repeated adjustments and modifications all scientists must engage in to make their experiments work. Instead, Sorensen refers to tinkering as a dialectical, and thus linguistic, procedure. This seems to point to a crucial difference between thought and empirical experiments: empirical experiments must conform to, indeed exist in, the external world, whereas thought experiments take us on a tour of possible worlds. Sorensen's experimenters tinker with the theories tested and/or discovered by experiments, not the experiments themselves. Unexplained anomalies arise, and (thought) experiments are conducted either to confirm or to refute the anomalies in an attempt to revise the old theory or construct a new one. This is the same kind of "theory first" discussion which the last decade's "new experimentalism"[6] in the philosophy of science has attempted to eliminate. Experiments in the physical world have an extra-linguistic life: microscopic images remain robust under changes in theory; meter readings and many other results survive radical conceptual changes. So, while thought experiments do not causally interact with their objects of study, as in most external-world experiments, I maintain that it is precisely this causal interaction which makes most experimentation in the external world epistemologically essential and which separates modern science from the neo-Aristotelian contemplation that Jonas seeks. As a result, thought experimentation remains a useful conceptualizing practice, but it can offer us no new knowledge beyond empirical experiments, bearing in mind the lessons of Mach's sensationalism; thought experiments rely on an empirical basis which, in fact, comes from experiments in the physical world.

Thought Experiments and Belief Systems

For instance, Hilpinen (1988) argues that experimentation is best viewed as a process of inquiry. Hilpinen's account can be understood in the relationship between belief systems, primary questions, secondary questions, and knowledge situations. A belief system can be conceived of as a system of accepted propositions that serves as the main product of investigative activity. In short, questions are asked, and thus experiments conceived, relative to belief systems, certainly not *in vacuo*. To paraphrase Pasteur, scientific discovery favors only the prepared mind.

Belief systems are assessed based on their ability to provide error-free answers to primary questions. A primary question addressed to a belief system expresses the questioner's desire that his/her belief system provide some satisfactorily informative answer (for example, Will the application of DDT pose harm to the environment?). Such an answer is defined as follows: "The system gives a satisfactory answer to a question Q only when the investigator knows some proposition p such that p is a complete answer to Q" (Hilpinen 1988, 18). This is the case only insofar as p is justified within the belief system; that is, it is true or at least highly confirmed. The belief system may not have a satisfactory answer, or it may even provide a contradictory set of answers. Hilpinen refers to such instances as knowledge situations, which are to be resolved with secondary questions. Knowledge situations include the following:

(a) B_a contains no (complete) answer to primary question Q;

(b1) B_a contains two or more conflicting answers to the same question; or

(b2) B_a contains an answer which is not justified within the system. (Hilpinen 1988, 23)

Hilpinen's claim is that secondary questions are asked as epistemic imperatives to fill in the empty spaces in a belief system or to resolve a certain contradiction within the system. Rather than directly addressing the question to the belief system, the questioner attempts to access "some external source of information. The source of information may be the investigator's own senses, a measuring instrument, an experimental apparatus, or any other source which is external to the investigator's own belief system" (Hilpinen 1988, 20). Thus, secondary questions, as epistemic imperatives, are experimental questions.

These experimental questions provide the baseline information for future thought experiments and future primary questions. Thus, while no experiment, thought or otherwise, can occur absent the belief system, thought experiments would be quite impossible without the external sources of information collected in secondary questions, for it is the answers to these questions which enrich the belief system and resolve its internal inconsistencies.

Jonas seeks a tool for modern technology in which all possibility is revealed. When all possibilities are revealed, particularly those damaging ones, a "heuristic of fear" can then be used to guide our actions. Recall that he has maintained that the imaginative value of the thought experiment is that it can foretell possibly harmful consequences which have no analogue to present experience. As I have argued, however, no thought experiment can reveal all possibility, for we will always be linked, to some extent, to our belief system and the past and present experiences contained within it. *Contra* Jonas, all thought experiments, then, have analogues in the past and/or the present.

The number of possible consequences of technological action is surely limitless, if we understand possibility as logical possibility. No human (or computer, for that matter) has the cognitive or computational capacity to consider such a search space. Thus, we can limit ourselves, even in thought experiments, only to those consequences judged to be feasible. Feasibility is determined in thought experiments, at least in part, by our experience in the external world—in short, through our ability to intervene in that world. Thought experiments, as a result, depend on our experimental/Baconian science, not a return to scholastic contemplation.

Conclusion

This discussion of Jonas and thought experiments offers a glimpse into the possibly fruitful alliance between applied ethics and the philosophy of science. The lesson would appear to be that the imperative of responsibility has both moral and epistemic dimensions. I do not quarrel with Jonas in the sense that thought experiments are both necessary and useful in both science and ethics. My concern is purely methodological. We need to be cognizant of the fact that only a deeply committed rationalist would believe that knowledge, with no analogue to past or present experience, is possible through the use of thought experiments. Tempered with a healthy dose of empiricism, we realize that our thoughts do have analogues to past and present experience, and thus so, too, do our thought experiments.

In the final analysis, Jonas's enthusiasm for the epistemic, and thus ethical, value of thought experiments rests on a misunderstanding of Aristotelian natural philosophy, which Jonas characterizes as "contemplative." Aristotle placed ample emphasis on the contemplative faculties, but he recognized the role of active intervention in natural phenomena as well. In Aristotle's metaphysics, the Forms exist within physical objects in the sensory world, not in some supersensory, Platonic realm. Consider the mutual dependence of mind and sense in the following: "The soul is analogous to the hand; for as the hand is a tool of tools, so the mind is the form of forms and sense the form of sensible things" (Aristotle 1931, book 3, 432a). This passage from *De anima* highlights both Aristotle's lingering Platonic rationalism, as well as his empiricism. His emphasis on the role of empirical experiments is crucial to understanding the role of sense data in his epistemology. For example, *Historia animalium* contains the earliest known systematic embryological experiments. Aristotle's chicken embryo experiments involved the actual removal of the eggshells at various stages in the embryo's development in order to view structural changes through time (Aristotle 1910, book 6, 561a3–562a20). Hence, Aristotle recognized the importance of intervening in nature if we are to understand it.

However, a problem which has always faced science is the investigation of those phenomena with which we cannot intervene. These include those beyond the realm of physical possibility, for example, the core of the sun, beyond the scope of current technology, and those which have yet to occur, that is, future events. The desire to investigate such phenomena led to the development of physical and mathematical models of phenomena, as well as the use of thought experiments. Jonas desires that thought experiments augment technology with a heuristic of fear, wherein the contemplation of imagined ecological disaster leads to more responsible action. Yet we must realize that thought experiments, as well as their automated cousin, the computer model, are limited in their ability to examine the vast search space of technological consequences.

There is perhaps no more excellently detailed analysis of the environmentally damaging consequences of improperly used mathematico-computer models than Shrader-Frechette's 1990 study of the ill-fated hydrogeologic modeling of the Maxey Flats radioactive waste site in Kentucky. The model employed at Maxey Flats predicted that waste plutonium would migrate less than one-half inch from the disposal site in 24,000 years. Considering that plutonium 239 has a half-life of 25,000 years, this would seem to be a prediction that the citizens of the surrounding areas could live with. However, within ten years of the site's 1963 opening, plutonium and assorted other radionuclides had migrated two miles from the site and into the surrounding surface waters.

While most of Shrader-Frechette's insightful analysis deals with the profound policy implications that result from inevitably flawed mathematical models (1990, esp. 92–108), it is her analysis of the inevitable link between such models and empirical data which is central to our present discussion. It is important to remember the composition of any mathematico-computer model. However, Klein explained, "Well, a model is first a data set, and then a set of statistically estimated equations, based on that data set. . . . And then today's model would also include the computer software . . . that would tell how to apply it, and in some cases solve it" (quoted in Judson 1987, 145). In this context "it" is the set of simultaneous equations which, in most cases, necessitates the use of high-speed computers instead of human brains to solve within particular scientific contexts. Truly, these are automated thought experiments. As Shrader-Frechette (1990) notes most explicitly, "Of course, the Achilles heel of the whole calibration and modeling process is the fact that no model, either in terms of its system assumptions or in terms of particular values for its parameters, can be validated. This is because of the inadequacy and inaccuracy of the data that are supposed to act as checks on the accuracy of the model." As it turns out, the hydrogeological models in the Maxey Flats case, and for that matter any computer model, were subject to the establishment of a set of initial conditions. The models in question were highly sensitive to measurements and, perhaps more crucially, estimates of soil moisture, soil porosity, and the relative prevalence of subterranean fissures. In the end, there is no doubt that such models depend on "real world" data and are no substitute for the ability to interact with that world. The same would apply for a discussion of econometric models, for they, too, depend on a set of antecedent data and assumptions, our problematic set A from above.

If our desire is to gain new knowledge of the physical world, thought experiments alone are an inadequate tool in and of themselves. In order to prescribe ethical behavior in the environment, it is clear that we must concentrate our energies in that environment itself, as well as with thought experiments. While we should utilize the conceptualizing power of thought experiments, we must recognize their epistemic limitations, a limitation set by our own experiences in the external world—the environment, which is the main topic of concern.

NOTES

1. Schramek (1980, 167) notes, "Ideally, industry should produce the greatest good for the greatest number of people." Schramek wrote that utilitarian line while serving on the executive committee of Ciba-Geigy, Ltd. The individual for whom the company is partially named, J. R. Geigy, was awarded a British patent in 1942 for a substance discovered seventy years earlier by the German chemist Zeidler. Its chemical name is dichloro-diphenyl-trichloroethane. DDT presents us with an example of technology's inability to predict all of the consequences of its projects. For nearly three decades, DDT was known as a miracle chemical. Its reputation as a chemical and technological savior from the ravages of insect-borne disease appears in a little known volume entitled *DDT: Killer of Killers* (Zimmerman and Lavine 1946), which details the beneficial consequences of DDT application. By the mid-1960s, however, it had become apparent that environmental metabolites of DDT, such as DDE, were carcinogenic materials. Clearly, most of the pre-1960 tests of human DDT toxicity dealt solely with acute, as opposed to chronic and carcinogenic, effects. Avian life such as the peregrine falcon and brown pelican became gravely endangered species during the heyday of the chemical's application, and no scientist predicted the threat posed by DDT-resistant insects that thrived after their cousins, which did not carry the trait of chemical resistance, perished without reproducing. Other examples abound of damaging and potentially

damaging consequences of seemingly well meaning scientific and technological actions in the environment. Flood control levees and walls designed to protect river towns from flood damage may actually alter the natural flood plain to the point that it takes less rain to bring damaging floods to communities down-stream that lack similar flood protection. Animal species introduced into new ecosystems for the purpose of pest control often breed out of control in the ab-sence of natural predators, becoming pests themselves. (The cane toads of Aus-tralia are a graphic example.)

2. I refer the reader to Kristin Shrader-Frechette's 1990 treatment of risk assess-ment in environmental ethics. Excellent accounts of the uncertainty involved in probabilistic scientific explanations can be found in Salmon (1967) and Howson and Urbach (1989).

3. G. Liebig concentrated on industrial and agricultural concerns at his Univer-sity of Giesen chemistry laboratory from 1820 through the 1850s. Liebig's concentration on quantitative analysis and the predictive powers of scientific chemistry spurred the growth of industrial chemistry in both Germany and Great Britain.

4. The 1992 Philosophy of Science Association meeting devoted a special session to thought experiments, and the 1992 publication of R. Sorensen's *Thought Experiments* reveals the importance of this issue.

5. This is also known as the "tacking paradox" or the "problem of irrelevant conjunction."

6. Ackermann (1989) coined this phrase. See also Ackermann (1985), Hacking (1983), Franklin (1986, 1990, 1992), Galison (1987), and Pickering (1989), to name but a few of the finer works in the philosophy of experiment.

REFERENCES

Ackermann, R. 1985. *Data, Instruments, and Theory: A Dialectical Approach to Understanding Science.* Princeton: Princeton University Press.

———. 1989. "The New Experimentalism." *British Journal for the Philosophy of Science* 40:185–90.

Aristotle. 1910. *Historia animalium.* Translated by D. W. Thompson. Oxford: Oxford University Press.

———. 1931. *De anima.* Translated by J. A. Smith and W. D. Ross. Oxford: Oxford University Press.

Ellul, J. 1972. "The Technological Order." In *Philosophy and Technology,* ed. C. Mitcham and R. Mackey, 86–105. New York: Free Press.

Franklin, A. 1986. *The Neglect of Experiment.* New York: Cambridge Univer-sity Press.

————. 1990. *Experiment: Right or Wrong?* New York: Cambridge University Press.

————. 1992. *The Rise and Fall of the Fifth Force.* New York: American Institute of Physics.

Galison, P. 1987. *How Experiments End.* Chicago: University of Chicago Press.

Glymour, C. 1980. "Hypothetico-Deductivism Is Hopeless." *Philosophy of Science* 47:322–25.

Hacking, I. 1983. *Representing and Intervening: Introductory Topics in the Philosophy of Natural Science.* New York: Cambridge University Press.

Hanson, N. R. 1958. *Patterns of Discovery: An Inquiry into the Conceptual Foundations of Science.* New York: Cambridge University Press.

Hilpinen, R. 1988. "On Experimental Questions." In *Theory and Experiment,* ed. D. Batens and J. P. van Bendegem, 15–29. Boston: D. Reidel.

Howson, C., and P. Urbach. 1989. *Scientific Reasoning: The Bayesian Approach.* La Salle, Ill.: Open Court.

Jonas, H. 1984. *The Imperative of Responsibility.* Chicago: University of Chicago Press.

Judson, H. F. 1987. *The Search for Solutions.* Baltimore: Johns Hopkins University Press.

Mach, E. 1984. *Contributions to the Analysis of Sensations.* Translated by C. M. Williams. La Salle, Ill.: Open Court.

Pickering, A. 1989. "Living in the Material World: On Realism and Experimental Practice." In *The Uses of Experiment: Studies in the Natural Sciences,* ed. D. Gooding et al., 275–97. New York: Cambridge University Press.

Rolston, H. 1988. *Environmental Ethics.* Philadelphia: Temple University Press.

Salmon, W. 1967. *The Foundations of Scientific Inference.* Pittsburgh: University of Pittsburgh Press.

Schramek, H. 1980. "Industry and the Environment." In *Ethics in an Age of Pervasive Technology,* ed. M. Kranzberg, 167–71. Boulder, Colo.: Westview Press.

Shrader-Frechette, K. 1990. "Models, Scientific Method, and Environmental Ethics." In *Upstream, Downstream: Issues in Environmental Ethics,* ed. D. Scherer, 90–120. Philadelphia: Temple University Press.

Sorensen, R. A. 1992. *Thought Experiments.* New York: Oxford University Press.

Zimmerman, O. T., and I. Lavine. 1946. *DDT: Killer of Killers.* Dover: Industrial Research Service.

MARKKU OKSANEN

Environmental Ethics and Concepts of Private Ownership

Should a landowner be free to alter his or her property in a manner that threatens the lives of those species living on it? How may people govern, and how should they govern their property in nature? What is at stake in environmental ethics is primarily the same as what is at stake in "the philosophy of ownership," that is, the moral relations that hold among humans and between humans and the natural world.[1] Both the rules of ownership and the principles of environmental ethics give liberties and dictate restrictions to the owners (as moral agents) in their dealings with the natural world. Therefore, a problem of adjusting potential and actual conflicts between these domains of norms arises inevitably, largely because the activities to which the ownership entitles the owner may be the kind of activities forbidden by the principles of environmental ethics. The conflict is about the content of ownership, by which is meant "the sum of all that can be done with it [the owned thing]" (Lawson and Rudden 1982, 8). There are different concepts of ownership, which means that there are disputes over the basic rules of ownership and how the concept of ownership may be modified, if it may in any way at all. Is it acceptable to think that property rights do not entitle the owner to promote the extinction of some population, or is the rule forbidding ecologically unsound action a justified "general background constraint" (Waldron 1988, 33)?

114

To Own, Not to Own, and How to Own

Many environmental ethicists have criticized the view that the natural world is primarily a property object; that is, to own a thing P is to make P an instrument to be used in any way that the owner sees fit. Aldo Leopold's famous passage on the land ethic indicates the environmentalist mentality as follows: "There is as yet no ethic dealing with man's relation to land and to the animals and plants which grow upon it. Land, like Odyssey's slave-girls, is still property. The land-relation is still strictly economic, entailing privileges but not obligations." [2]

Leopold's suspicious attitude toward regarding the natural world solely in economic terms appears understandable when considered in an appropriate historical context. The traditional rhetoric of ownership in seventeenth- and eighteenth-century liberal thinking used to merge the metaphysical ideas of human superiority and human dominion over nature with the individual's right to property so that dominion was embodied in people's efforts to cultivate their lands and to coerce their lands into more productivity. John Locke, for instance, in the important chapter "Of Property" in his "Second Treatise of Government," tells a story about the earth as God's present to humans in common, how God commanded humankind to subdue the earth and to make use of it as they saw fit, and how what was left unlabored should be considered wasteland. [3] Even more symptomatic is Sir William Blackstone's characterization of private ownership as "sole and despotic dominion which one claims and exercises over the external things of the world, in total exclusion of the right of any other individual in the universe." Similarly, he also relies on the Christian story of how "the all-bountiful creator gave to man 'dominion over all' the earth; and over the fish of the sea, and over the fowl of the air, and over every living thing that moveth upon the 'earth.' This is the only true and solid foundation of man's dominion over external things" (Blackstone 1966, 2–3).

So when the despotic, characteristically anthropocentric, and deeply religious worldview was questioned by the early environmentalists, ownership seemed to be in a position of losing some of its moral and metaphysical justifiability and in need of reconsideration. Although it is usually acknowledged that property rights, in a sense of being absolute, are impossible and have occurred hardly ever in any legislation (Honoré

1987, 187–90), the idea has been appealed to and the discourse has been employed in opposing any environmental regulation that sets limits on the right to use.[4] (The environmentalists also have used this fact to establish some historical legitimacy and credibility for their argument and for that of private ownership.) Therefore, the main target of environmentalist criticism has been this concept of property rights. As a response, the property rights position has become "a rallying cry these days for the antienvironmental movement" (Freyfogle 1994, 481). The conservatives allege that any environmental regulation with regard to real property, such as zoning rules, "would represent a movement away from the private property principle towards one of common or socialist property" (Wagner 1993, 13) or would constitute a taking requiring an appropriate compensation (Epstein 1985). For them, the environmentalist challenge seems to be mainly "the battle over who should control the land" (Paul 1987, 14).

The environmentalists are seriously attempting to rest their views on ethical principles. Those who advocate a biocentric or an ecocentric environmental ethic would find it difficult to grasp the proper subject of moral concern in nature as an object of property and, thus, subject to any treatment whatsoever. Individualistic biocentrism, to put it simply, says that certain natural entities have moral considerability similar to that of human beings, and we have a duty not to violate their basic interests without appropriate reason (see, for example, Taylor 1986). The idea of unsuitability of nonhuman living beings to be property items is based on analogical reasoning (although this is seldom pointed out explicitly): if humans as moral beings—whether or not they are moral agents—are not something that may be owned by other humans, it would be inconsistent to hold morally similar nonhuman beings as objects of property.

For holistic ecocentrists, such as those who give to the land a Leopoldian meaning and who consider some "wholes" as morally considerable, ownership in a sense of absolute dominion over the land is an unsatisfactory moral position. In Aldo Leopold's land ethic, the notion of land has a special moral significance. It refers not to the mere soil but to the whole community of life and its physical conditions. A human being is a plain member of the land community, and the moral obligation is to acknowledge this fact in one's mental life and behavior directed at the natural world (Leopold 1987, 204). This view implies the existence of certain restrictions in the right to use resources the way there are restrictions in our behavior toward other people.

However, from a realistic point of view, human beings inevitably have to arrange their social relations regarding the natural world, which implies the emergence of property regimes in every society.[5] Accepting this premise, what could be a sound basis for owning natural resources except something that is compatible with the basic environmentalist values, that is to say, a system of rules and practices likely to prevent, for example, human-caused degradation, unnecessary suffering of sentient beings, diminished biological diversity in the natural world, and the sustainable use of renewable resources simply to protect nature's good. The standards of justifiability of the modes of ownership depend on how they serve the environmentalist goals. How does private ownership meet this requirement? And if it does not prove to be the best conceivable social arrangement, are there any better alternatives, and what mixture of property systems would be environmentally ideal? As a critical starting point, we should keep in mind that an assumption concerning the existence of an institution of ownership does not mean that a universal system of private ownership as known in libertarian literature is the only alternative.

Despite these tensions between the environmental and property rights movements, there are those who defend property rights on ecological grounds, as well as environmentalists who believe property rights and environmental duties are not necessarily contradictory. Although they all may accept the private property system (to a certain extent),[6] one point of difference is about the *conceptions* of ownership. We may distinguish between two basic conceptions of how to reconcile environmental values with (private) ownership in nature: unqualified and qualified. The fundamental difference lies in how the concept of ownership is to be defined.

The unqualified view holds that the owner decides how one is going to treat and make use of one's property without violating similar rights of other people. Ownership grants permission provided one does not cause any harm to others. This view is most ardently defended by libertarians and neoclassical economists—and some of them have renamed their position as free market environmentalism.[7] As their starting point, they believe that humans are self-interested beings by nature and that economical rationality is to be conceived in terms of self-interestedness. The private property system is believed to harness the self-interested humans

to use their own assets in a way that (invariably) accords with the environmentalist principles and goals. The owner knows best his or her own interest, the customer's interest, and how to satisfy both in an optimal way
without violating others' rights and without acting against environmental ends (see Hardin 1977a, 2; Anderson and Leal 1991, 4). Instead of regarding private property as an obstacle to environmental policy, the advocates of the unqualified concept think of it as a necessary institutional
device. A socially and ecologically problematic situation arises when no
property regimes exist, because in such a case "there is no delimitation
or delineation of its use rights to any private party" (Cheung 1987, 504).
Paying most attention to the issue of free access—or, as the economists
controversially call it, the commons—they claim that private ownership
is ecologically superior to other modes of ownership and also superior to
the situation of no ownership. They think that the exploitation of natural
resources outside all institutional settings is worse than that of utilizing
them within an economy based on private ownership.

According to the qualified view there are some other restrictions, *besides* the basic requirement of not harming others, which regulate the use
of one's property. There may be for the owner a set of requirements to fulfill either positively or negatively. There are many variations. In the moral-
ist account presented by Aldo Leopold (1987, 209), ecologically sound
use of one's land depends on one's moral outlook, by which a person does
not consider the issues of land use merely as a matter of how to accomplish self-interested economic goals. Leopold's institutional solution was
not that of abolishing the property institutions but rather redefining them
on the basis of a new, nondespotic worldview. He stated that "an ethical
obligation on the part of the private owner is the only visible remedy for
these situations," largely because he was worried about the state's ability
to carry out everything important in environmental preservation (1987,
213–14). Whereas Leopold does not say explicitly that these ethical obligations should be legalized, his adherents nowadays are clamoring for a
shift from the unregulated and unqualified conception to the regulated
and qualified conception of ownership in legislation (see Freyfogle 1990,
1993; Karp 1989, 1993). Generally speaking, those environmentalists
who are not radically in favor of alternative property arrangements and
economic systems not built mainly on private ownership have been of the
opinion that the state may regulate the use of one's property and, in cases

of preserving some ecosystems or species, the state should take control of them. In their account, social regulation, in the sense of restricting and directing an owner's activities, and confiscation by the state constitute the basic means of an environmental policy. The policy has been implemented so extensively that it has led some observers—whether they are critical or not—to point out that, overall, regulation has nearly put an end to land as private property as we have known or imagined it (Varner 1994, 158). This notice is particularly interesting, since it brings forward the question of ownership: If the content of ownership is qualified, can we still say that one truly owns something?

The basic issue, then, seems to be whether there are specific rules in any set of property rights that regulate the use of one's property in a substantial way or whether the content of ownership is to be left unqualified and decisions on the use of one's property in the owner's sole authority. Simply put, instead of speculating on whether or not to own, we should ponder how to own. In case 2 above, the content of ownership is qualified to satisfy the environmentalist's requirements, and in case 1, this movement away from the absolutist ideals is deemed unnecessary, if not contrary, to the fundamental Lockean principles of private ownership, which, if enforced properly, could alleviate ecological problems. The further we go in analyzing the concept of property, the less evident it becomes that Richard Epstein's assertion about the commonly shared meaning of property rights among its defenders and its contenders is accurate (Epstein 1985, 25).

It is also plausible that the limits of activity are wider and that the protection of property rights is stronger in the unqualified than in the qualified position. How those positions are related to the environmentalist causes will be considered next in more detail as I assess their prospects as the basis of an adequate environmental policy.

The Concept of Ownership as Unqualified

To begin with the concept of private ownership as unqualified, one cannot neglect John Locke's defense of property rights. It has been said that the most specific Locke has been on the concept of ownership is the following: "I have truly no property in that, which another can by right take from me, against my consent." [8] Locke seems to suggest that any regulation would require the consent of the owner to be justified; whenever the owner has not consented and given up consciously some of his or her rights, no intervention may occur. This quotation suggests that the "true essence" of ownership is that the use of property is solely up to the owner. In an earlier passage (sec. 4), Locke states that there are some limits (namely, the laws of nature) which could be understood to imply the acceptance of intervention. Yet, making things more complicated and sensitive to interpretation, Locke introduces two conditions for appropriation. The conditions known as the Lockean provisos (secs. 27–34) dictate that what God has given to humans in common should not be wasted and one should appropriate property in nature provided that there is enough and as good left for others. (I shall not examine the political and moral meaning of these provisos in this essay.) What Locke really meant by ownership has been closely examined in the literature of political philosophy throughout this century, just as the dispute has raged over the concepts of private property between the traditional capitalist-bourgeois and the welfare-state capitalist interpretations of Locke. The former interpretation stresses private ownership as unqualified, and according to the latter view Locke's theory of property is "enough to support restriction of certain property rights in natural resources like land" (Shrader-Frechette 1993, 201). One interpreter situates himself between these positions and claims that "the Locke that emerges from his theory of property is . . . pluralistic and moderate" (Simmons 1992, 222). Locke's texts bear monumental political significance, and as they are open to different readings, they attract fierce political debate.

In the libertarian reading on Locke, the aspect of the owner's authority is strongly emphasized. Stripped from all religious tones, this conception of property rights entitles the owner to decide about the use of property autonomously. The conception is unqualified. By this I mean what Ellen Frankel Paul has expressed: "At the very heart of the property rights conception—that what is mine may be used by me as I see fit provided only that I not use it in a manner that violates the like right of other owners" (Paul 1987; cf. Epstein 1985, 59–60). The libertarian interpretation on Locke stresses that property rights are natural rights, which means, as John Simmons (1992, 223–24) has put it, "its binding force is nonconventional and it could be possessed in the state of nature." What Locke seeks is a secure and protected concept of property rights, which could only be actualized when the legitimacy of property rules is not regarded as consensual, conventional, or legal, because those conditions make them subject to the constraints of society.

In addition to the historical foundations to advocate the unqualified position, there is some analytical support for it. Tony Honoré (1987, 162) has characterized ownership as "the greatest possible interest in a thing which a mature system of law recognizes," which seems to leave the content of ownership to the law. In his analysis of standard incidents of ownership, however, Honoré characterizes the right to use property as "a cardinal feature of ownership." Although there are some modes of activities that are not allowed to be undertaken, "the standard limitations on use are, in general, rather precisely defined, while the permissible types of use constitute an open list" (Paul 1987, 168; cf. Epstein 1985, chap. 5).

We can distinguish between at least two kinds of ecological arguments for private ownership, the teleological and the deontological. In the teleological argument, environmental preservation is explained as occurring through the owner striving for his or her long-term interests. The nature and content of these interests are believed to coincide with the fundamental values of environmentalism. The deontological argument is grounded in a reflection of how abstaining from activities that harm other people's interests and their property advances environmentalist goals. In this ecological argument for unqualified property rights, the institution in itself harnesses people to behave in an environmentally sound way.

Teleological Argument

The teleological argument for a private property system is a mixture of the Aristotelian defense of private property and the view of human nature advocated by neoclassical economists. According to the argument, the efforts of the self-interested owner are believed to bring about the environmental values simultaneously with individual well-being. The argument is explicitly based on an assessment about the consequences of the private property system it carries to the natural world.

Probably the most important ecological argument of the teleological kind is presented by Garrett Hardin in his famous 1968 narrative on "the tragedy of the commons." Although Hardin's political solution sometimes has been characterized as "centralized authoritarianism" (O'Riordan 1976, 305–6), and although he recognizes some limits to and even some problems in "the private property solution,"[9] he should be regarded as a strong advocate of privatization of the common property resources.

The argument that land will be in a better condition under private ownership than under communal or state ownership is an ancient one. It can be found in Aristotle, who wrote, "The greater the number of owners, the less the respect for common property. People are much more careful of their personal possessions than of those owned communally; they exercise care over common property only in so far as they are personally affected" (Aristotle 1962, 1261b32, 108). Grunebaum (1987, 37) has found two main reasons for Aristotle to favor private ownership: motivation and knowledge. Hardin seems to represent his argument in the same way as Aristotle, even if with some modifications.

The point of departure in Hardin's theory is the worry about the deterioration of "the commons," which is caused by an aggregate of human actions. By the term *commons* Hardin—following the standard but controversial use of the term in economics—refers to the land and natural resources that are freely exploitable outside social constraints for any human or a group of humans.[10] Under these circumstances, due to a lack of any external (state) and internal (voluntary) control, individuals are trying rationally to maximize their profits in using the commons as efficiently and as promptly as they can. As a result of all people self-interestedly and rationally doing the same, these resources will be overused. If an agent is going to get as much as others or anything at all, it is rational to strive for immediate utility and, thus, to unintentionally bring closer the ruining of the commons forever. This is the predicament that Hardin calls "the tragedy of the commons."

Hardin believes that if the natural resources existing outside all normal property arrangements were under private control, they would be used and managed in an ecologically sound manner. The owner would then be in a position to prohibit others from using what belongs to the owner, and the owner alone could freely concentrate on taking care of and using the assets as seems best. As soon as it is possible for the owner to exclude others, it becomes rational to seek profit maximization in the long run. The idea of expected and durable advantage would operate as an incentive, and by virtue of that, the agent would take care of what is owned, or it would be rational to take care of it. It is in one's self-interest to ensure that one also will get a living from the land in the future and that there is a supply for future markets as well. When one is aware of this, one is motivated to be concerned about one's property (Cf. Rothbard 1978, 248). This point emerges in Hardin's writing: "Under a system of private property the man (or group of men) who own property recognize their responsibility to care for it, for if they don't they will eventually suffer. A farmer, for instance, if he is intelligent, will allow no more cattle in a pasture than its carrying capacity justifies. If he overloads the pasture, weeds take over, erosion sets in, and the owner loses in the long run." [11] Hardin rejects neither the concept of rational behavior as self-interested behavior nor (psychological) egoism in morals. Instead of challenging these ideas, he argues for institutional change (1977a, 43), for the privatization of the commons: "Moralists try to solve problems like this by denouncing 'selfishness' and 'greed'; but denunciation is seldom any good" (Hardin 1977a, 39).

The final argument to prove the goodness of the private property system is based on the gathering and transfer of information. Hardin compares modes of ownership. Two alternatives turn out to be better than others, namely, socialism and what he calls "privatism." As seen above, the owner can be motivated to manage property in nature without jeopardizing the meeting of future needs. The knowledge the owner possesses can be characterized as direct and unmanipulated by virtue of the close relations between the owner and the owned thing. In socialism, Hardin believes, "the advantage of position gives managers first whack at the statistics, which they can alter or suppress to hide evidence of their incompetence" (1977a, 37). With regard to the control issue, Terry Anderson and Donald Leal repeatedly criticize the selfishness and irresponsibility of bureaucrats and the inefficiency of the socialist alternative. They think that bureaucrats can be selfish freely and transgress the laws because there is nobody to watch them. It is my view that irregularities on the part of the bureaucrats are possible, but they are not necessarily tyrants beyond judicial control; there are citizens to watch them and laws to prohibit unaccepted modes of behavior. The existence of social problems is not a sufficient counterargument. What the last point means, as I understand it, is similar to what Anderson and Leal (1991, 4–5) have written about more clearly, namely, the significance of knowledge required for efficient stewardship and decision making: "Free market environmentalism sees a much smaller knowledge gap between the experts and the average individual [than centralized political resource management system]. In this view, individual property owners, who are in a position and have an incentive to obtain time- and place-specific information about their resource endowments, are better suited than centralized bureaucracies to manage resources." Anderson and Leal describe the private property system quite unrealistically because they ignore the existence of big land owners, the enterprises whose turnover might be bigger than that of some nation states. If the information problem is to be resolved, then the land ownership should be small scale and close to the land.

According to the teleological justification for property rights, outlined above, private ownership in nature prevents "the tragedy of the commons." Nothing much is said about the content of ownership, but the emphasis on the owner's ability to manage resources more rationally than communities or states presupposes that the owner has sole authority over his or her property. It is supposed that the external enforcer does not know how to manage the resources as well as the owner.

Does this arrangement protect what it is supposed to protect? In my opinion, it is inadequate and misleading for certain reasons. I shall consider it not in light of empirical surveys made on the existing system of the commons[12] but in light of the compatibility of its axiological underpinnings and practical expectations.

The impasse of the teleological argument occurs in unification of human self-interest and nature's good. This may be too trivial to say, but it is simply nonsense to think that human self-interest without any qualification whatsoever invariably coincides with nature's good or with the sustainable use of natural resources. If we (for the sake of the argument) ignore all social and economic pressures, the ecological results of this institutional arrangement are entirely contingent on what the owners see as their best interest. What is good for the owner may not be good for environment, and vice versa. To illustrate this difficulty, let us consider a case of protecting rare plant species located on private land. If it is entirely up to the owner to decide how to benefit from his or her land, the deliberation may or may not result in the preservation of the species. But in order to arrive at an outcome of preservation of the species and to convince any opponents, the free market environmentalist has to prove through a calculation of the utility values of each option what is the most advantageous manner of use. If we assume that the owner is motivated to gain profits from the property, the problem is the following: "To think that property rights can be a basis for conservation is to assume that conservation of resources is more profitable than any other investment that might be made with gains from immediate consumption" (Sagoff 1981, 301). Anderson and Leal (1991, 21) say that "measuring, monitoring, and marketing the land for endangered species habitat requires entrepreneurial imagination." It surely requires a lot of imagination to show someone how to make money from the resources that one cannot use or the use of which is restricted definitionally.

Hardin presupposes self-interest, which means that if the aim for preserving the natural world for the good of all humanity conceptually cannot be the major end of singular self-interested acts, then it must be a secondary aim, and it occurs by definition as a by-product, alongside the primary acts motivated by pure self-interest. This implies that preservationist aims have to be something that will be realized automatically. How this could happen is mysterious. For these reasons, I conclude that the teleological argument for private property as the only acceptable system of ownership and for the privatization of the commons is not convincing.

Deontological Arguments

Deontological arguments as ecological arguments for the private property system emerge from a strict interpretation of the harm principle. All the others ideally are excluded from affecting one's own property. Any harm inflicted on others, that is, any act violating the claim of excludability, requires consent from the party being harmed and, if requested, decent compensation. The owner has a duty not to take up harmful uses (Honoré 1987, 174), and the endeavor to avoid causing harm constitutes the primary tactic of this type of libertarian environmental policy. The reasoning is implicitly based on an assumption that prohibition of acts harmful to others is to coincide with those acts that would be harmful to the natural world. (In this sense, the argument is by nature both anthropocentric, since the beings who are being harmed are supposed to be humans, and deontological, since the criterion to assess the deeds is not that of the consequences.)

Their concept of ownership is clearly unqualified, and there are no qualifications concerning the content of ownership. The only legitimate reason why others or the state may interfere with the autonomous position of individuals and corporations in the use of their own property is where the principle of nonharming has been violated: an interference for any other reason would violate rights of persons unjustifiably. As Ellen Frankel Paul (1987, 234) writes, "The only relevant considerations, from a rights viewpoint, are who has a right to what, and who aggresses against that rightfully owned thing." In other words, the notion of property rights functions in itself as a delimiting factor regarding the use of the things fallen into ownership.

Imagine a libertarian utopia in which all nature and natural resources on earth are divided into shares, and each share is owned by an individual who has procured it, without violating any of the acquisition rules. Each individual is entitled to use his or her share as each pleases and sees as economically profitable as long as others are not harmed. When the harm is unavoidable—and this fact has been recognized generally by all parties in society—there are two questions: Should that sort of behavior be allowed or not? And if it is permitted, on what terms should it take place?

There is a logical possibility that the whole industrialized society as we know it lies on an unjustified basis. Assuming that the pollutants a factory emits into its neighboring areas are instances of intervention, assuming that any intervention without the owner's permission is harmful, and assuming that any harm is prima facie unjustified, then if any party being harmed requires that the harmful activities and processes be stopped, there is a case for these activities and processes to be stopped. This is acknowledged by both critics and proponents of the libertarian view. As libertarian Murray Rothbard points out,

> The vital fact about air pollution is that the polluter sends unwanted and unbidden pollutants—from smoke to nuclear fallout to sulfur oxides—*through* the air and into the lungs of innocent victims, as well as onto their material property. All such emanations which injure person or property constitute aggression against the private property of the victims. . . . The major function of government—of courts and police—is to stop aggression; instead, the government has failed in this task and has failed grievously to exercise its defense function against air pollution.[13]

And Andrew McLaughlin (1993, 34) writes,

> Such an absolutist view of property rights has a strange consequence—industrial society is morally illegitimate! This is because pollution is an inevitable result of many industrial processes. Air pollution, for example, inevitably spreads beyond the property of the polluter. Factories, as well as automobiles, pollute the air breathed by others. It is difficult to imagine industrial processes that export *no* pollution. Such pollution erodes the property rights of those who are unwillingly subjected to it.

Hardly any libertarian would be willing to accept this implication, since they are generally spokespersons for the blessings of economic growth[14] and would be unlikely to start arguing for the closure of polluting plants. In spite of Anderson and Leal's attempt, the critics have characterized their ideology as thoroughly anthropocentric, which "stands in stark contrast to the ecocentric orientation towards which most greens lean" (Eckersley 1993, 9). By not taking a serious attitude toward this possibility of green policy on their own terms, libertarians and neoclassical economists are rather willing to compromise their basic principle for the other values they endorse.

One solution not conducted by the government is presented by Ronald Coase, who in his acclaimed article, "The Problem of Social Cost," depicted the problem of side effects as reciprocal: "The question is commonly thought of as one in which A inflicts harm on B and what has to be decided is: how should we restrain A? But this is wrong. We are dealing with a problem of a reciprocal nature. To avoid the harm to B would inflict harm on A. The real question that has to be decided is: should A be allowed to harm B or should B be allowed to harm A? The problem is to avoid the more serious harm" (Coase 1960, 2). According to Coase, the economically active party also would have to suffer from not being allowed to undertake these harmful activities—but in what sense is the party harmed? One noteworthy issue in Coase's thinking is its peculiar understanding of the harm principle. It has been noticed that "the principle that one ought not to harm others seems to be ignored by Coase" (Hanly 1992, 78). In other words, the possibility that B will absolutely refuse to stand the harms caused by A seems not to have been taken into account as a feasible prospect. But to have such a concept of harm—that anything the nonactive party deems as harmful constitutes harm of the sort which compels the active party to forbear from his or her activities—is not a plausible and realistic concept of harm. Surely we have to stand some things that we dislike and that violate our interests. The problem of what kind of harm to others is to be tolerated is a complicated issue. What are the basic elements of harmful use? What sorts of harms are wrongs? Who has the burden of proof to show whether or not one has been harmed and, if one has been harmed, just how harmed?

However Rothbard regards Coase's presumption, the two writers' solutions are alike: both rely on the use of the courts and the legal structure (Rothbard 1978, 260). It is questionable whether or not this model implies any environmental policy. The mode and extent of it depends on several factors; for instance, on how the court interprets the concept of harm and what are the final results of bargaining between all parties involved. Assuming rather unrealistically that the conflict is bilateral, and the parties, both economically active, concede to a mutual right to harm, the harms caused will be eliminated, but only when it comes to these humans and not to the natural environment. Nevertheless, Coase's solution may be incorporated into environmental policy as in the case that follows.

The other rationale says that if some sorts of harm are permitted but subjected to compensation, it would be more profitable to minimize the amount of the harms because of their costs. The reasoning for how private rights may regulate the use of property goes as follows: If it is rational for a human owner to act according to self-interest, and if the owner is liable to compensate for the harm caused to others' property, then the owner is likely to abstain from causing any harm to others and to their property because the nuisance can be costly.

To argue for the importance of a private property system, we have to suppose that all of nature has been divided into private ownership. Therefore, if a private property system obtains, there is no uncompensated pollution, that is, there is no free and uncostly harming of others' property. If we assume that nature should be harmed as little as is possible, it is justified to divide nature into shares and to distribute those shares among humans as items of private property (according to some principles of justice and property acquisition), because this arrangement functions as a delimiting factor in human behavior regarding the use of nature.

It is plausible that the deontological libertarian strategy to protect the natural environment will provide us with a policy that works to a certain extent but not well enough. There are some insuperable obstacles, both theoretical and practical. First, is it possible to restrict the use of one's property in such a manner in which the use does not cause any harm to others or their property but is ecologically unwise? The answer is negative because the rigid enforcement of property rights also implies that other people are not allowed to interfere with any of the owners' nonharmful activities. Second, as we have seen earlier, negotiations between persons or corporations about the price of the inflicted harm do not ensure directly in every case what would be environmentally good. Third, as a matter of fact, the libertarians do not hold strictly to the principle of nonharming, but rather they agree that it can be overridden in some cases; otherwise, it would require too much or deny something they appreciate. And in any case, the conflict of interests would be won most plausibly by those having the best capacity to display evidence favorable to them. Fourth, the question of the right to carry out environmentally risky and hazardous plans is even more puzzling, if not unsolvable; there are simply cases where the cost of damages and injuries of possible accidents is far too high for any private party and thus is to be carried jointly. The case is puzzling because individual parties may take measures that they know are beyond their capacity to make up the losses, but it is possible that full liability may make people give up hazardous activities.

In summary, the ecological results of this policy are in many cases contrary to fundamental environmentalist goals. For a concerned environmentalist, pure faith in market mechanisms and in owners' arbitrary decisions just makes one restless if one is not permitted to work for what one believes is right and worthwhile on all levels that a democratic society allows.

The Content of Ownership as Qualified

Property rights can be nonharmful regarding our environmentalist goals. One option to attempt to achieve this goal is to define the content of ownership to coincide explicitly with these aims and principles, and any violation of or deviation from the basic environmentalist principle would be deemed an abuse of one's property. This sort of general sense of private ownership is qualified, since there are other conditions of the legitimate uses of a property item besides the harm principle. I sympathize with this concept of private ownership even though I recognize certain difficulties in the views elaborated.

The nature of qualification of ownership can be negative or positive in the sense that some modes of behavior regarding the owned things are not accepted or that some positive acts are required to be performed. The harm principle as depicted in the libertarian conception is in kind a typical negative rule: the owner is entitled to everything that does not transgress the harm principle. The qualification is positive when the goals that the owner is constrained to pursue are more or less explicitly defined. What has been most commonly required is the achievement of certain quantities in production; then the standards dictating that the owner seek economic growth can be unfavorable from the environmentalist's standpoint. The requirement can be expressed more inexplicitly in terms of "good husbandry"[15] or "a duty of land stewardship" (Karp 1993, 748). The latter expression can be explained, for example, in terms of sustainable use of one's land resources to produce a certain amount of goods without spoiling its productive capacity. A characteristically environmentalist guideline could propose, for instance, that the landowners should not diminish the amount of diversity of species living on their land. This guideline may consist of both negative and positive rules depending on how human activity affects the state of biodiversity in the area. There are cases where the inactivity may increase or preserve the number of species (as in the case of not cutting down the old forests) as well as where activities of the right kind may lead to the same result (as in the case of not giving up pasturing a meadow). Although it is difficult to deem positive control like this as a brute case of taking, the attitude among mainstream property rights advocates toward the qualifications is generally not too positive: "Such arrangements present the form but not the substance of liberal ownership" (Honoré 1987, 191). Richard Epstein (1985) labels such a social arrangement as a "partial taking" that constitutes a threat to the "unity of ownership."

Another distinction that we can make among the defenders of the qualified property conception is to classify them into two categories according to their philosophical methods and their philosophical justification for ownership: instrumentalists and noninstrumentalists. The instrumentalists think that private property rights may be forced to operate for whatever socially chosen end, such as those of the common good or general happiness. To accomplish the ultimate aim that society as a whole is presumed to endorse, the content of ownership can be defined as having such constituent rules that contribute to the chief aim. This has been a more typical way to approach the issue of justifying the plans of environmental protection in cases where private ownership collides with larger social interests and is outweighed by them.

The concept of ownership held by the noninstrumentalists is restricted and qualified on a logical basis: for them private ownership includes no such rule that entitles one to ecologically unsound use of property, and "to own" is always to own within given limits that are inherent in the very idea of ownership.

Robert Goodin has chosen the latter strategy, and he attempts to show that the system of private ownership does not necessarily conflict with environmentalist values. Goodin claims that those who oppose the preservationist policy cannot ground their resistance on the idea of property rights because there is no such specific right as "a right to destroy" in the most coherent set of property rights that could be violated by preservationist policy. Therefore, the owner is not entitled to treat the plot of the natural environment in a destructive way; property rights and our duties toward the natural world are compatible. This also implies that the "green political theory" can be realized without overruling the institution of private property (Goodin 1992, 108).

The task Goodin imposes on himself is to find some support for his claim that "there seems to be no analytic reason to suppose that property rights entail a right to destroy" (Goodin 1990, 417). His point of departure is Frank Snare's quite constricted 1972 analysis in which three *principal* components in the notion of property rights are separated. Goodin also admits (following Snare) that some other particular rights and duties might be regarded, but leaves this aside from his analysis because of their lesser significance.

According to Snare, what the language user means when he mentions that "A owns P" is the following:

1. A has a right to use P. (The right to use.)
2. Others may use P if, and only if, A consents. (The right to exclusion.)
3. A may permanently transfer the rights under rules 1 and 2 to specific other persons by consent. (The right to transfer.)

As we see, in Snare's list there is no mention of the right to destroy when this specific right is understood to be the antithesis of a preservation policy. To find out whether there is a hidden "right to destroy" in any of these components and what we could mean by that concept, he considers them individually and collectively without finding such a right. The nonexistence of this specific right implies that some other reasons exist in addition to the harm principle for intervention, namely, in cases of exceeding the limits that the ownership authorizes the owner to operate with regard to the owned thing. These limits make the regulation of ownership cover more than just inflicting harm on others.

Goodin's argument for delimited and qualified ownership of property item P is the following:

> To say merely that you have a right to use something is to say that you have a right *merely* to use it. To say that you have a right to use something, and to say no more than that, constitutes an implicit withholding of permission for you to do more than to use it. The clear implication of saying that you have a right to use it, and saying no more than that, is that you have *no* right to destroy it. To destroy it would clearly be doing something more than merely using it, and that right has been implicitly denied you. Through such reasoning, something rather like a duty to leave things as you found them can be derived from rights (merely) to use things.

Goodin adds that if this is true, then "not only will it have shown there is no necessary conflict between property rights and preservationist duties; it will have shown the former actually entail the latter" (Goodin 1990, 410).

In fact, Goodin's view is logically even stronger than the view requiring avoidance of destruction, since there is a positive condition imposed upon the owner. He says that "'a duty not to destroy' is itself implicit in a *mere* 'right to use.'" It means that ownership in P does not give permission to destroy P and implies that if one cannot use one's property without destroying it, then one has to abstain from using it (Goodin 1990, 410, 412). According to this interpretation of property rights, the owner loses some of the freedom that libertarians are willing to attribute to the owner regarding the things in ownership. The advocates of the unqualified position would tend to attack this conception of ownership by alleging that it dismisses the true essence of ownership. They may notice that Snare's analysis lacks the right to capital and to income,[16] which could conflict with Goodin's concept of ownership.

Although Goodin's argument is interesting from the environmentalist point of view, there are some problems. For one thing, I am sure that Goodin's proposition would frighten landowners, because it does not take for granted the legitimacy of compensation paid in cases where the prima facie rights to use, management, income, and security—all the specific rights that conflict with preservationist duties—have been over-ruled by the state. If the exercise of the above-mentioned incidents of ownership are not made intrinsically permissible in ownership and if they do not belong to any list that comprises the owner's liberties, there is no reason why the owners ought to be compensated for their claims that they do not, in fact, legitimately hold. This is an implication too radical, I think, to make Goodin's concept of ownership socially viable. It will fail for the same reason as the conservative's claim that in all the cases of regulation, however insignificant it is, some compensation is required legitimately.

Second, I believe defining property rights and rules is still at least as much a matter of political decision making as it is that of pure conceptual analysis. We may account the content of ownership without paying much attention to the logic of the concepts. (In the end, it might be the case that the content of ownership is as much a result of conceptual analysis as it is a decision based on value considerations.) What does Goodin mean by asserting that one may not destroy what one owns?

The deficiency of mere conceptual method becomes more concrete in illustrating what the verb *to destroy* means to different cultures. Consider a Finnish example. Large areas of Finland are marshlands. Therefore, it is no wonder that a bog traditionally has been a wasteland for a farmer, and its cultivation has been appreciated because farmland has been a scarce resource. However, for a concerned ecologist, a bog is a valuable ecosystem with an exceptional diversity of species. This implies that it should not be altered. Today both mental images of marshlands are alive. If the farmer intends to utilize the wasteland and drain it, it would be a destruction mainly for the biologist and not for the farmer; and what is unwise waste of potential farmland for the farmer is preservation of a biological treasure for the ecologist. Who is to say where destruction takes place? A more recent controversy, comparable with the bog example, is whether or not the old-growth forests should be allowed to be cut. In this dispute people are interpreting the notion of "destroying" in incompatible ways. There are people who feel that if we do not exercise clear-cuttings in an old-growth forest, we leave the trees to decay; we waste these resources and, in that sense, destroy them. The preservationist would be of the opinion that devastation would occur if the forests were exploited.

What is destruction in the cases depicted above? What kind of activities may the owner undertake? The conceptual analysis does not yet give definitive answers to this problem. What Goodin is essentially trying to do is to move the issue about the content of ownership into a new discourse, but to define certain types of use as destructive does not necessarily bring any solution. Destruction is a culturally varied concept. The interpretation of it, even in a culturally homogeneous country such as Finland, would be troublesome.

Let us consider a bit further the question of logging the forests. It is probable that a certain number of trees may be cut and some lumbering is acceptable, but if we have a general concept of destruction covering all these cases, we are left to choose between two options: a cut in the forest either is an act of destruction or it is not. But what should be maintained is a view that neither logging in general nor abstention from logging in general constitutes destruction. What a reasonable environmental deliberation would require is that the decision should be made upon a deliberation that is more sensitive to contextual matters, where some logging and some preservation are accepted.

A question rises: Is it so that the content of ownership is contextual, at least in one sense, depending on the nature of the thing owned? And if so, what kind of rules of ownership should be applied to different items of property? Could such rules be constituted so that the treatment depends on the moral status of the property item (does it have intrinsic value or is it aesthetically irreplaceable)? And if so, who is to decide the moral status of objects, and who should be authorized to define the rules of appropriate treatment of those objects? If the practice of ownership changes dramatically, how should the people suffering from these changes be compensated justly? And finally, what is an environmentally optimal allocation of property? If some form of the qualified position were accepted, as I hope, there is still an immense task to clarify what it means in different situations. The criticism I am directing at Goodin's view arises mainly from his belief that a pure conceptual analysis would bring us to a solution in a problem that is not purely conceptual. The qualified conception of ownership is likely to create a good basis for an environmental policy that would satisfy the environmentalist prerequisites, but it needs further qualification.

Conclusion

The institution of ownership is basic to every society that determines how people are to use natural resources. This institution divides external nature into shares, and each share is governed by individuals, by communities, or by nations. It is striking that property theorists, whether they are philosophers, political theorists, economists, anthropologists, or lawyers and regardless of their political views, agree to a great extent on the most general level of the logical analysis of the meaning of the term *ownership*. They may hold to a view that ownership is something that endows the greatest possible authority to decide about the use of one's object of property. But what are the limits of one's authority? There is hardly any consensus in praxis among the group mentioned above.

The ecological argument for private property says that private ownership is not contrary to environmental preservation but a necessary institutional condition for it and that human self-interest can be harnessed to promote environmental preservation, but only within this arrangement. What it requires is that property rights are clearly defined and strongly enforced; however, the content of ownership has been left unqualified. I have concluded that the environmental policy practiced under these social settings, by nature, would be accidental. Therefore, the case for free market environmentalism or "ecological libertarianism" does not stand up to critical reflection.

I have not given any argument against private ownership in general. Rather, I have claimed that there are no ecological reasons to prefer one single system of ownership to others and to see it as a necessary institutional arrangement in resolving ecological problems. It follows that in the global marketplace, the tendency to transact merely in liberal terms should not be the only one. Second, determining ownership rules so that they are ecologically sound cannot be done in general terms. If the institution of ownership is submitted to environmental consideration, it will bring no easy solutions: to build the environmentally sound institutions of ownership is a task that will not be completed as long as there are humans.

NOTES

I am grateful for the linguistic assistance of Marjo Rauhala-Hayes.

1. On the idea of environmental ethics see Taylor (1986, 2–3); on defining ownership this way see Grunebaum (1987, 4).

2. Leopold (1987, 203); see also Blackstone (1974, 39) and McLaughlin (1993, chaps. 2–3).

3. Locke (1963, secs. 25–51). See environmentalist commentaries: Sagoff (1988, 171–94); Hargrove (1989, 64–73).

4. There are many national debates on property rights and environmental regulation. On the debate in the United States, see Echeverria and Eby (1995). In Finland, Kultalahti's 1990 dissertation generated a debate.

5. Grunebaum (1987, 20–24). By supposing the necessity of systems of ownership, and thus refuting the possibility of an anarchist society without such systems, I do not intend to claim anything specific about what kinds of natural beings may appropriately be property objects.

6. The issue of range of property items is interesting in terms of both human and environmental ethics: What are the things in the world one may own? Should all local economies that have thus far remained outside the capitalist world economy be replaced by a liberal or a libertarian system of private ownership?

7. The book by Anderson and Leal (1991) bears that title.

8. Locke (1963, sec. 138). Quoted in Grunebaum (1987, 4).

9. Hardin (1968, 1245). In "Discriminating Altruisms" (1985, 186) Hardin supports cooperation between individuals: "People often must act in concert (generally, though not necessarily, through government) to bias the free enterprise system so that self-interest becomes congruent with public interest."

10. Hardin (1977a, 30). It is claimed by several authors that Hardin misuses the concept of the commons both historically and conceptually. For a critical summary see Aguilera-Klink (1994).

11. Hardin (1977b, 264–65). Cf. Anderson and Leal (1991, 4).

12. Evidence of the viability of the nonprivate property system is shown in Feeny et al. (1990).

13. Rothbard (1978, 256–57); cf. Machan (1984, 97).

14. See, for example, Rothbard (1978, 246–47); the index of Anderson and Leal (1991) does not have such a phrase as *economic growth*.

15. This requirement was imposed upon cultivators by the British Labour government in 1947; see Goodin (1990, 401) and Honoré (1987, 191).

16. See the standard incidents of liberal ownership listed by Honoré (1987, 165–67).

REFERENCES

Aguilera-Klink, Federico. 1994. "Some Notes on the Misuse of Classic Writings in Economics on the Subject of Common Property." *Ecological Economics* 9:221–28.

Anderson, Terry L., and Donald R. Leal. 1991. *Free Market Environmentalism.* San Francisco: Pacific Research Institute for Public Policy; Boulder, Colo.: Westview Press.

Aristotle. 1962. *Politics.* Translated by T. A. Sinclair. Harmondsworth: Penguin Classics.

Blackstone, Sir William. 1966. *Commentaries on the Laws of England.* London: Dawson of Pall Mall.

Blackstone, W. T. 1974. "Ethics and Ecology." In *Philosophy and Environmental Crisis,* ed. W. T. Blackstone, 16–42. Athens: University of Georgia Press.

Cheung, Steven N. S. 1987. "Common Property Rights." In *The New Palgrave Dictionary of Economics,* ed. John Eatwell, Murray Milgate, and Peter Newman, 504–5. London: Macmillan.

Coase, Ronald. 1960. "The Problem of Social Cost." *Journal of Law and Economics* 3:1–44.

Echeverria, John, and Raymond Booth Eby, eds. 1995. *Let the People Judge: Wise Use and the Private Property Rights Movement.* Washington, D.C.: Island Press.

Eckersley, Robyn. 1993. "Free Market Environmentalism: Friend or Foe?" *Environmental Politics* 2:1–19.

Epstein, Richard A. 1985. *Takings: Private Property and the Power of Eminent Domain.* Cambridge: Harvard University Press.

Feeny, David, Fikret Berkes, Bonnie J. McCay, and James M. Acheson. 1990. "The Tragedy of the Commons: Twenty-two Years Later." *Human Ecology* 18:1–19.

Freyfogle, Eric T. 1990. "The Land Ethic and Pilgrim Leopold." *University of Colorado Law Review* 61:217–56.

———. 1993. "Ownership and Ecology." *Case Western Reserve Law Review* 43:1269–97.

———. 1994. "Owning the Wolf: Green Politics, Property Rights, Ecology Rights." *Dissent* (fall): 481–87.

Goodin, Robert. 1990. "Property Rights and Preservationist Duties." *Inquiry* 33:401–32.

———. 1992. *Green Political Theory.* Oxford: Polity Press.

Grunebaum, James O. 1987. *Private Ownership.* London: Routledge and Kegan Paul.

138 MARKKU OKSANEN

Hanly, Ken. 1992. "The Problem of Social Cost: Coase's Economics versus Ethics." *Journal of Applied Philosophy* 9:77–83.

Hardin, Garrett. 1968. "The Tragedy of the Commons." *Science* 162:1243–48.

————. 1977a. *The Limits of Altruism: An Ecologist's View of Survival.* Bloomington: Indiana University Press.

————. 1977b. "Living on a Lifeboat." In *Managing the Commons,* eds. Garrett Hardin and John Baden, 261–79. San Francisco: W. H. Freeman. Reprinted from *Bioscience* 42 (October 1974): 10.

————. 1985. "Discriminating Altruisms." In *Deep Ecology,* ed. Michael Tobias, 182–205. San Diego: Avant Books.

Hargrove, Eugene. 1989. *Foundations of Environmental Ethics.* Englewood Cliffs, N.J.: Prentice Hall.

Honoré, Tony. 1987. "Ownership." In *Making Law Bind: Essays Legal and Philosophical.* Oxford: Clarendon Press.

Karp, James P. 1989. "Aldo Leopold's Land Ethic: Is an Ecological Conscience Evolving in Land Development Law?" *Environmental Law* 19:737–65.

————. 1993. "A Private Property Duty of Stewardship: Changing Our Land Ethic." *Environmental Law* 23:735–62.

Kultalahti, Jukka. 1990. *Omaisuudensuoja ympäristönsuojelussa.* [Constitutional property rights and environmental protection]. In Finnish, with English summary. Jyväskylä: Finnpublishers.

Lawson, F. H., and Bernard Rudden. 1982. *The Law of Property.* 2d ed. Oxford: Clarendon Press.

Leopold, Aldo. 1987. *A Sand County Almanac and Sketches Here and There.* New York: Oxford University Press.

Locke, John. 1967. "Second Treatise of Government." In *Two Treatises of Government,* ed. Peter Laslett, 266–446. Cambridge: Cambridge University Press.

Machan, Tibor. 1984. "Pollution and Political Theory." In *Earthbound: New Introductory Essays in Environmental Ethics,* ed. Tom Regan, 74–106. Philadelphia: Temple University Press.

McLaughlin, Andrew. 1993. *Regarding Nature: Industrialism and Deep Ecology.* Albany: State University of New York Press.

O'Riordan, Timothy. 1976. *Environmentalism.* London: Pion Limited.

Paul, Ellen Frankel. 1987. *Property Rights and Eminent Domain.* New Brunswick, N.J.: Transaction Books.

Rothbard, Murray N. 1978. *For a New Liberty: The Libertarian Manifesto.* New York: Collier.

Sagoff, Mark. 1981. "Do We Need a Land Use Ethic?" *Environmental Ethics* 3:293–308.

————. 1988. *The Economy of Earth: Philosophy, Law, and the Environment.* Cambridge: Cambridge University Press.

Shrader-Frechette, Kristen. 1993. "Locke and Limits on Land Ownership." *Journal of the History of Ideas* 54:201–19.

Simmons, A. John. 1992. *The Lockean Theory of Rights.* Princeton: Princeton University Press.

Snare, Frank. 1972. "The Concept of Property." *American Philosophical Quarterly* 9:200–206.

Taylor, Paul W. 1986. *Respect for Nature: A Theory of Environmental Ethics.* Princeton: Princeton University Press.

Varner, Gary E. 1994. "Environmental Law and the Eclipse of Land as Private Property." In *Ethics and Environmental Policy: Theory Meets Practice,* ed. Frederick Ferré and Peter Hartel, 142–60. Athens: University of Georgia Press.

Wagner, Richard E. 1993. "Parchment, Guns, and Constitutional Order." In *Property Rights and the Limits of Democracy,* ed. C. K. Rowley, 1–75. Aldershot: Edward Elgar.

Waldron, Jeremy. 1988. *The Right to Private Property.* Oxford: Clarendon Press.

DAVID SKRBINA

The Ethics of Free Trade

The approval of NAFTA and the World Trade Organization (WTO) by the U.S. government seriously undermines efforts at moving society toward environmental sustainability. The very process of free trade leads to accelerated resource depletion, absentee ownership, loss of local control, and the disempowering of people everywhere. Accountability is moving into the hands of international corporations who may be driven to unethical practices by factors beyond their control.

Since free trade manifests itself as orienting economies toward greater consumption of imports and greater production of exports, I conclude that the rational and ethical course of action is to reduce imports and exports significantly.

The federal government has an ethical obligation to restrict free trade policies and to protect businesses that decline to compete internationally. Corporations are obliged not only to "buy American" but to sell locally as well. And consumers have the responsibility to buy locally made goods and to consider global implications of purchase decisions. In the past few years, the issue of free trade has come to dominate the business world, and it has become a major concern of our federal government. The passage of NAFTA and the WTO promises to alter the global business climate by greatly increasing the volume and nature of international trade. In this essay I will focus not on the economic merits of free trade but on the cultural, environmental, and philosophical tradeoffs. There are serious ethical implications for business and government, and I hope to expose the inherent difficulties arising from increased international trade.

A Common Moral Stand

First, we need to build a bridge. Opponents of free trade typically have been in one of three groups: environmentalists, farmers, or labor unions. Farmers and unions protest on the basis of self-preservation; they see their livelihoods threatened. Environmentalists oppose trade for a different reason. They act not out of direct self-interest but out of greater concerns for the health and well-being of people everywhere and for the nonhuman world and its intrinsic worth. Environmentalists fear that free trade will hasten resource depletion, increase pollution and waste, and drive down standards for protection to the lowest common denominator.

Those supporting free trade include most senior corporate officers and the majority of our federal legislators. They argue that free trade means more jobs, a greater standard of living, and a stronger economy. A strong economy, they claim, is better able to pay for such things as environmental protection.

Environmentalists and corporations take a similar but opposing stand when debating the merits of global commerce. Both see themselves as custodians, as stewards, of something precious: environmentalists of the earth, and businesses of capital. Both nature and capital are vital to society. Both are deserving of protection.

Similarly, each party sees the other as a threat. Business leaders view environmental restrictions as a cost burden and an inhibitor to their competitiveness or even as an attempt to put them out of business. Environmentalists see the pursuit of capital and profit as causing inevitable damage to the ecosystem.

Thus environmentalists and corporate executives claim the high moral ground. They both seek to fulfill their responsibility to preserve and protect a valuable commodity, and they see themselves as performing a right and necessary social role. As a result, charges by each that the other is being irresponsible and even immoral can seem hollow and contradictory, at least to the average citizen listening in on the debate.

Both sides care deeply about humanity and its future. Both parties consist, for the most part, of honest, dedicated, compassionate people. It is important to acknowledge this fact and to avoid demonizing members of either group. This step must come first. Mutual derision furthers no one's cause.

Having acknowledged these points, we are compelled to ask if the two opposing allegiances can be reconciled. I hope to show that commerce in itself is not necessarily a problem, but that extensive global trade can be disruptive to the well-being of our planet. Here the issue of free trade becomes important; it vividly illustrates the conflict between capital and nature and raises the stakes of the entire debate.

I will consider now three important aspects of free trade: the disruption of social organizations, the disempowering of communities, and negative repercussions of economic growth.

Social Disruption

Free trade means far more than simply producing more goods to sell overseas. It leads to significant and continuous restructuring of the supplier/producer network. New markets are invaded, prices are driven down, and "inefficient" local producers are driven into bankruptcy. This turbulence results in a corresponding upheaval of numerous local business regions, which disrupts the lives of employees and others who depend on stable business conditions.

A free trade world is clearly not a stable one. More and freer trade translates into greater competition. Our former "non-free" system had plenty of competition, but now we are embarking on an era of true cutthroat competition, affecting nearly all aspects of our manufacturing sector.

Cutthroat competition is an ugly sight. It leads to a desperation mentality, wherein actions are taken to ensure one's survival. It can lead to irrational or suicidal behavior, as real or perceived threats appear on the horizon—think of the "suicide pill" of excessive debt that some companies take on to fend off hostile takeovers, or selling products below cost to maintain market share, or laying off employees to reduce costs. It pushes corporate managers to the edge of moral and legal behavior, because they know that, under many circumstances, if they don't do it, someone else will.

Excessive competition also effectively prevents business from implementing progressive workplace policies. If some company should choose to reduce its work week, increase pay, improve health benefits, provide flexible work hours, or do any of a variety of innovative worker-friendly practices that raise costs, some international competitor will likely forego such luxuries. International competition acts to drive down employee quality-of-life standards, which significantly affects social well-being.

Employees engaged in cutthroat competition are not happy. They are under stress, they are asked to produce more for less money, and they have fewer corporate amenities to make the job more bearable. The pressure reflects back on their family lives, contributing to numerous social problems. And, of course, those who get laid off are even less happy; they must find a new job and often move their family in the process. Social stability goes out the window.

Free trade economies are highly fluid; they accept continuous change as a modus operandi. Free trade proponents acknowledge this disruption, but counter that it is part of a short-term restructuring of the economy. They imply, but do not explicitly claim, that this restructuring will result in long-term stability. Unfortunately, virtually no theoretical or empirical evidence supports this conclusion.

Communities need to be stable social organizations. People do not like continuous change. Social bonds cannot develop with people constantly moving in and out or with rapid swings in the relative prosperity of communities. By its very nature, free trade will inevitably accelerate change.

Loss of Self-Determination

Another major social effect of international trade is loss of self-determination. Congressional opponents have rightly argued that NAFTA would erode U.S. sovereignty as transnational corporations and multinational trade commissions acted in their own best interests rather than the nation's.

Sovereignty erodes further as our economy becomes increasingly dependent on other nations. Consider the recent debacle of the Mexican currency bailout. A mere twelve months after NAFTA, our economy was so closely linked to that of Mexico that 700,000 jobs were imperiled by the peso devaluation, and we required a $20 billion loan package, authorized by presidential executive order, to support Mexico's currency (and contribute to the decline of our own). One easily can imagine this trend progressing to the point where our national security is jeopardized by some foreign trading partner, at which time almost any action could be justified by Washington.

Equally important to erosion of national sovereignty is the issue of local control (at the city or state level) of a community's environmental and business conditions. Free trade means more products, more manufacturing, more business decisions controlled by corporations in other nations. This necessarily means less input by citizens affected by these business decisions.

It seems that every day we hear of plant closures, layoffs, or job transfers that devastate a neighborhood or small community. The community may plead with the company to reconsider. They may voluntarily offer to accept wage cuts. Sometimes they will even initiate a lawsuit, usually without success. All this from American companies. How much worse will it be with increasing foreign control over our economy?

Empowerment is a hot term in business these days. Companies are realizing that empowered workers are more satisfied and more effective. So too with the citizenry. Empowered citizens who have a strong voice in local business decisions and in environmental tradeoffs are certainly happier, healthier, and more productive than those who work at the whim of some distant corporate headquarters. And free trade will unquestionably increase the pervasiveness of distant control.

Self-determination is the fundamental right of society. It is the foundation for every form of democratic rule. Local business activity and the condition of the local environment are key aspects of self-determination. People everywhere deserve the right to have substantive influence over these conditions. Free trade, without a doubt, will decrease this control and therefore is counter to the core human right of self-determination.

The Dark Side of Economic Growth

Free trade is certain to increase economic growth. And we all know growth is good, right? Can growth really solve all our economic, social, and environmental problems? It seems that most economists and politicians today would have us believe so, and they therefore steer our nation along this path.

Economic growth is becoming increasingly difficult to maintain in the

United States, which is why businesses are looking to foreign markets for expansion. For example, auto sales have peaked around 13 to 14 million vehicles per year, and the growth in the number of vehicles on the road has slowed to zero for the first time ever (there is approximately one vehicle on the road in the United States for every person over the age of sixteen). With minimal population growth in this country, American businesses can achieve sales growth only in other nations. This need for continuous growth is a significant motivator of the free trade agenda.

In the simplest terms, we may think of the global economic system as one in which raw materials are extracted and converted into consumer goods. These goods are used, exchanged for other goods or services, and then discarded as waste. Waste is also created in the extraction and conversion processes.

Without delving too deeply into the matter, I would like to point out a few basic aspects of economic growth. One, growth inevitably means continued, if not increasing, consumption of natural resources. Between 1980 and 1990, the real per capita GDP in the United States increased 18 percent. In that same period, total wood and lumber consumption rose 20 percent, coal consumption rose 30 percent, and total energy consumption rose 23 percent. Consumption of metals and other nonmetal minerals has generally increased less than the GDP, but remains at high levels relative to the rest of the world. It appears certain that economic growth necessarily means more extraction, more consumption, and more waste.

Even if we assume limitless underground resources, the environmental damage caused by extraction continues, as does the energy use and pollution caused by processing. And as production gradually moves out of the United States, other countries (typically the poor ones) increasingly absorb the degradation and pollution. This fact alone is a strong moral indictment of free trade. How can we justify environmental abuse of third world citizens who may be poorly informed and often have no voice in such actions?

Two, growth cannot continue indefinitely. Growth has occurred on and off throughout history, as human needs and ingenuity have increased. But the global economic system was allowed to grow because the effect was small compared with the total earth ecosystem. After centuries of growth, we are beginning to reach the limits of a finite ecosystem to supply raw materials and to absorb pollution and waste.

Limitless growth is a physical impossibility on a finite earth. The sooner we adapt our economic system to this reality, the less painful and the less damaging the conversion will be.

Three, growth is a difficult process to manage, and this process becomes exponentially harder as the system gets larger. Our little U.S. economy, a mere $4.8 trillion, is itself beyond the grasp and understanding of mortal humans. We cannot predict its future nor can we control it, despite Washington's best efforts.

In a free trade world, the U.S. economy gets bound up further in the global economy. As the global economy grows, the complexities increase by orders of magnitude. Currencies rise and fall, markets soar and collapse, and capital moves at lightning speed. Contemplating the recent plunge in value of the U.S. dollar, German economist Rudolf Hickel exclaims, "Economists should concede that they simply can't explain the fall of the dollar." National governments find themselves unable to control their own economies. Gernot Nerb, director of the Institute for Economic Research in Munich, asserts, "The [national] central banks are powerless against the currency-market forces." And then consider the recent, dramatic case of twenty-eight-year-old investment banker Nick Leeson, who single-handedly bankrupted one of the oldest and most venerable banks in England. What better indication that a high-speed global economy is already beyond rational control and understanding?

These three points form a strong indictment of the pro-growth lobby. The lobby likes to counter that growth is actually good for the environment in that it allows us to pay for cleanups and new "green" technology. They point to recent improvements in the United States and Western Europe and to ecological destruction in the former Soviet bloc. This argument sounds rather like an alcoholic who needs just one more drink to work up the nerve to quit. We are so addicted to growth and high technology that we believe they can cure all ills, even those caused by growth itself.

The Basis for Corporate Ethics

Corporate ethics are driven by both internal and external factors. The primary internal factor is the company's statement of values and guiding principles, which presents the company's reason for being and formally acknowledges its core objectives. These values and guiding principles may be explicitly stated, as they are at Ford Motor, for example, or implicit in the day-to-day operation of the business.

The impact of values and principles is in turn affected by the determination of senior management to implement them. Values must be backed up by internal actions to communicate and educate. Also, corporate structure can determine how values and principles are implemented. A highly centralized and hierarchical corporation is linked by the direct control of subordinates and thus is less likely to need a formal statement of values or principles. In a decentralized company, guiding principles may be the only link to unify diverse suborganizations in a common purpose and vision.

The primary external factors are the profit incentive, absentee ownership, and limited liability. Profitability is the primary measure of how effectively and efficiently a company executes its business plan. Profits allow a monetary return to be paid to the owners of the company, typically the stockholders, who expect profits and will reclaim their investment (by selling stock) if anticipated profits are too low.

In most modern corporations, stockholders are absentee owners, having little or nothing to do with daily business decisions. Corporate employees typically do not own more than a small percentage of the total stock. With no direct connection to the way the corporation operates, these absentee owners become interested only in the short-term return on their investment and not on any long-term effects that the business may have on society or the environment.

U.S. law exempts stockholders from personal liability for anything that the company may do wrong. At the first hint of trouble, stockholders sell. They may sell for a loss, but beyond that they have no further equity in the corporation. Even in the extreme case of bankruptcy, stockholders may receive some portion of their investment, and in any case they are not held responsible for the actions of corporate officers.

Collectively these internal and external factors pose a troublesome contradiction for corporate ethics. If we think of the corporation as a "pseudo-person," then we may say that the internal values and principles represent his "good" side (integrity, high quality, socially concerned, etc.) and the external factors represent his "bad" side, which seeks short-term gain with little or no responsibility for wrong behavior, not unlike each of us.

Which factors prevail? I conclude that the larger the corporation, the more the external factors dominate. Small businesses, those with sales less than $100 million, have at least an equal chance to follow internal values as to be driven purely by profit motives. Large, complex, diverse corporations, however, appear to be driven almost entirely by the external factors. In spite of their best efforts and intentions, in spite of the integrity and compassion of the senior management, large businesses inevitably yield to maximization of profit and return on shareholders' investments. When it comes to such a conflict, internal values lose virtually every time.

This point of understanding is critical for all parties involved. Until we can strengthen internal corporate values or weaken the external forces, I fear we have little hope for improvement.

Who will address the larger problem of weakening these external factors of profit incentive, absentee ownership, and limited liability? This is the largest and most difficult challenge we face. Being out of the hands of business, it falls to society as a whole—the citizens and all levels of government—to reexamine this basis of our system of economics and commerce. An economic system that permits and encourages the unethical practices we have discussed clearly needs significant restructuring. This process will take much discussion and many years of effort, but we can certainly begin by taking a few modest steps in the right direction.

What Corporations Can Do

The challenge to us all is to find specific ways to encourage business to act in the larger interest of society and the environment. Let me offer up a few suggestions, beginning with some actions that corporations can take.

Clearly state internal values and guiding principles. These must be widely circulated. They must have the clear support of top management. And they must be reinforced with follow-up training and awareness classes. These principles should include at least one statement on personal integrity, one statement on social concern, and one statement on environmental concern.

Decentralize corporate management structure. This act not only allows a more efficient and effective business operation but it gives diverse business units the ability to implement the guiding principles in ways most appropriate for their situation. Stress that the corporate values are the common link throughout the company.

Work with the federal government to discourage free trade policies, even if this means introducing import quotas or tariffs. And if our trading nations retaliate by doing the same, then we must accept it in the name of a rational and just economic system. We must be willing to forego growth in foreign markets to retain self-determination.

Minimize the corporation's free trade practices to the extent possible. Buy only from American suppliers. Sell primarily to American markets. Avoid the temptation to expand into foreign markets. As the American economy and society benefit from this, so too will the corporation.

Admittedly, these are only small steps in the right direction. I do not claim that they will completely solve the problem at hand. As we have seen, there is a limit to what corporations themselves can do, because much of the problem lies beyond their control.

Implications for Government

Washington has an ethical obligation to discourage free trade. The federal government has a hand in setting and approving rules of international trade and thus is obliged to consider the larger ramifications. Congress approved NAFTA and the WTO largely in response to intense lobbying by corporate and pro-business interests, with support from pro-growth economists. This is a strong condemnation of Washington's ability to act in the true long-term interest of society. It demonstrates the pre-eminence of economic growth over all other social goals, to the detriment of the fundamental rights of self-determination and local control, and it shows Washington's uncaring attitude toward increased abuse of the global environment.

Also, government at all levels must support efforts to educate the public about all consequences of free trade. The corporate lobby and conservative media do a good job of promoting the financial benefits of free trade, and their resources overwhelm the smaller voices of opposition. Government is charged with protecting the public interest, not with making a profit, and it is clearly capable of supporting an informed citizenry.

The best way to facilitate public understanding of economic consequences is to decentralize the system. We should push economic responsibility for taxation and spending down to the lowest levels possible. This allows optimal local decisions to be made, where the consequences are more quickly and clearly understood. Our present economic system is too opaque to be understood by most economists, not to mention the average citizen. It must be made more transparent, more comprehensible, if it is to function rationally in a democratic society. Interestingly, the recent "Contract with America" drafted by congressional Republicans seems to be moving us in the right direction, even though it is motivated by other considerations.

Finally, we need leaders to show wisdom and courage in making the right decisions. Too often our leadership caves in to special interests, to short-term financial gain, and to popular initiatives. Vice President Al Gore promised to protect the environment, but he seems to have been subsumed by the larger forces of Washington. Leaders are, after all, expected to lead. Where else can society look for vision and guidance? Corporate executives? Writers? Entertainers? Surely not. Political leaders have a special obligation, and they need to step up to the task.

Consumer Responsibility

Consumers clearly share in the responsibility to stem free trade. In our market-driven economy, millions of daily consumer choices collectively create our business climate.

An informed consumer is one cure for economic policies gone astray. As I have mentioned, though, in a system as large and complex as ours, where the effects of individual choices seem so distant in space and time, it is difficult to expect the average consumer to make the most rational choice.

Perhaps more important than an informed consumer is an enlightened consumer, one who understands the deeper ethical implications of all business decisions. People who look only at the price of things tacitly support a system in which profit is of singular importance. An awareness of ecological values, especially frugality, can help guide consumers to make wise decisions.

As it is, we can never really know about the circumstances surrounding imported goods. Those cheap toys made in China may have been made using forced labor; these fresh fruits may have been grown in a cleared rain forest, using tons of pesticides and herbicides; this inexpensive suit may have been tailored in a foreign factory that eliminated one hundred jobs in some small American town. There are so many uncertainties about imported goods that almost nothing can be purchased with a clear conscience.

Given the concerns over free trade, the obvious recommendation is to buy American whenever possible. I realize that it can be difficult to define "American-made" these days, but in many cases the choice is pretty clear. If a product is designed and manufactured in the United States by an American-owned company, then the American content is obviously high. Japanese automakers who pitch their cars as "built in the U.S.A." are clouding the issue. The design work is still done in Japan, and the profits ultimately go back to Tokyo.

One other thing consumers can do is avoid investment in foreign companies. Overseas mutual funds are hot these days, but investing capital in foreign business is clearly not the way to encourage local business activity. Investments such as tax-free municipal bonds would certainly be much more appropriate for supporting local economies. People need to take the time to learn about free trade economics and the damage it can do. They need to understand what they give up for financial gain.

Conclusion

I can hear the criticism of my thesis already. "Prices will go up!" "American business will stagnate!" "Consumers have the right to buy whatever they choose!" "The Japanese will eat our lunch!" To these I answer, sure, prices will be higher than they would be with free trade, but the higher prices buy us something: they buy economic stability, social stability, self-determination, and environmental protection.

And I do not deny the right of a consumer to buy what he chooses. But when the economic system is so large and complex that he is virtually unable to make a wise decision, then the right to choose becomes an illusion.

Change is inevitable. Progress will continue. Competition is useful in rooting out inefficiency. People will always want to buy goods at the lowest possible price. I accept all these propositions. But we cannot allow the damage caused by inherent short-term consumer or stockholder self-interest to go unchallenged.

It is the fault not only of the consumer or stockholder. The system has grown so large, and its effects have become so distant and long-term, that the average person cannot be expected to grasp all the implications of his or her actions. We are all responsible for creating a more decentralized, more transparent economic system. Only this can allow people to begin to make wise decisions.

Free trade promises us economic success, but instead it delivers social disruption, uncontrolled and irrational economic systems, and loss of self-determination. It accelerates the global consumption of natural resources and gives increasing license to powerful, distant, profit-seeking entrepreneurs who inevitably act counter to the best long-term interests of the planet. These are the inevitable consequences, and for this reason global free trade must be morally condemned as an injustice to nature and humanity.

DOUG DAIGLE

Globalization of the Timber Trade

Regardless of their ecological differences, all of the world's forests are now joined in a single global market. For those concerned with saving native forests, it is vital to understand not only patterns of development that affect ecosystems but also the flows of trade that connect and fuel these patterns. The process of globalization can be seen most clearly in the Pacific Rim, where both the world's fastest growing economies and the bulk of its remaining forests are to be found. (It is understood here that *forests* refers to native forests, which includes both old-growth or virgin forests and second-growth areas that have an indigenous natural character as opposed to an intensely managed one.)

Transformation of the Timber Trade

Two major shifts have occurred as a result of globalization of the timber trade, a process marked by increasing centralization of the timber industry into a smaller group of large transnational corporations. The first shift in market dominance has been a replacement of raw logs by wood chips and pulp. Spectacular growth in the wood fiber trade—an increase by more than 300 percent since 1960—has been matched by a surge in pulp processing. In 1960, wood chips amounted to less than 10 percent of the fiber trade; by 1990, that amount had risen to 54 percent (Hagler 1993). Wood chips are particularly advantageous for ocean trade, where the economics of shipping favor pulp and chips over raw logs, even when the latter are ridiculously cheap, as in Canada.

This shift has developed in tandem with the industry's move from tropical to temperate and boreal forests as major sourcing areas. "Substitutability" of wood for pulp and chips allows comparable utilization of different species from different forest types. Nigel Dudley summarized this development in his report, *Forests in Trouble,* compiled for the World Wildlife Fund in 1992: "Changes in the structure and technology of both forestry and timber utilizations are causing major changes to the ways in which forests are used. In general, manufacturers can use a far wider range of species, ages, and qualities of trees, and demand is moving away from timber to pulp and cellulose. The increasingly international market means that new areas of forest are continually being utilized."

The attention of both the timber industry and environmentalists has shifted north to the forests of Canada, Siberia, and the United States, even as the situation in most tropical forests grows more dire. The greatest remaining supplies of timber lie in the boreal Siberian taiga, which alone accounts for 20 percent of global forest cover (Rosencranz and Scott 1992). Temperate forests, covering 2 billion hectares and providing half of global forest cover, are now among the most intensely logged areas in the world.

Substitutability of wood and the increasing ease with which the timber industry can shift the locations of its operations have also fueled fears about the sustainability of forestry and local timber–dependent economies. These trends and the fears that they engender are direct results of the globalization process.

Globalization and the Pacific Rim

In addition to containing the bulk of the world's remaining native forests, the Pacific Rim is home to its fastest growing economies. Most of these, such as China and the southeast Asian "tiger" economies, are responding to their acute timber shortages by rapidly increasing imports of wood products. Two-thirds of world trade in wood fiber takes place in the Pacific region, which is a base of operations for many of the key players in the timber industry.

In the view of timber analyst Alistair Graham (1993), "The economic development patterns in the countries of the Pacific Rim will largely determine the fate of remaining native forests both temperate and tropical, both hardwood and softwood." The forests of the Pacific Rim fall into the three broad global groups—tropical, temperate, and boreal—and, of course, into many more specific categories. A survey of their status vividly demonstrates the impacts of globalization.

Tropical Forests

Tropical forests in the Pacific Rim include those of Indonesia, Malaysia, the Philippines, and Papua New Guinea (PNG). Since the Second World War, the timber industry has been particularly hard on them. Overcutting has turned one nation after another into a supplier of raw logs and then an importer, as its forests have been depleted.

The evolution of timber exploitation in the tropical Pacific, like that of its economic development, has been driven largely by Japan (Nectoux and Kuroda 1989). Japan earned hard currency in the 1950s by importing hardwood logs from the Philippines and exporting processed timber products to the United States. In the Philippines, Ferdinand Marcos made a substantial part of his fortune by selling off his country's rain forests, similar to the way that later timber magnates have enriched themselves in Malaysia and Indonesia.

Japan turned to Indonesia and Malaysia after Philippine forests were depleted during the 1970s and 1980s. With the entry of South Korea and Taiwan into the Pacific Rim timber market, countries with less extensive areas of forest, such as Australia, Vietnam, Thailand, and Myanmar, have suffered significant impacts. Even countries with limited forested areas, such as the Solomon Islands, have come under increased pressure. The volume of logs exported has almost doubled in the last two years ("Eight Years Left" 1994).

Japan and South Korea have now shifted attention to Papua New Guinea. A spectacular worldwide rise in log prices in 1993 led the PNG government to approve a 400 percent increase in log export volumes. Little of the revenues stay there, but the government has nonetheless allocated two-thirds of "operable" forests for harvesting, despite growing local opposition.

The role of Japan and its neighbors in the tropical timber trade essentially has been colonial: areas rich in natural resources are harvested for processing and sale in distant centers of production and demand. This colonial character has been a hallmark of the global timber trade as well.

Temperate Forests

Figures from the U.N. Food and Agriculture Organization suggest that the actual area of temperate forests is holding steady, but this ignores the crucial issue of forest quality: many native forests are being replaced with intensely managed, monocultural tree stands, with a resultant loss in biodiversity (Dudley 1992).

Temperate forests in the United States and Canada have suffered severe impacts over the past decade by the expanding Pacific Rim market in wood fiber, especially for pulp and chips. These forests also have been the scene of some of the most intense social conflicts that have arisen from the timber trade. The largest instance of civil disobedience in British Columbia's history has occurred at Clayoquot Sound on Vancouver Island, one of the last extensive tracts of the coastal temperate rain forest that once reached unbroken from Canada to northern California.

Public attention in the United States was focused on the "owls vs. loggers" issue in the Pacific Northwest, which was, of course, not the real issue at all. Increased mechanization in the timber industry coupled with exports of raw and minimally processed logs caused the number of timber jobs to fall even during periods of record harvest. Timber employment fell 14 percent overall from 1980 to 1988, while production levels increased by 19 percent (Dudley 1992).

Events in the Northwest are also indicative of the fluidity with which the timber industry can move its operations. The domestic American industry has moved much of its production to the Southeast following the depletion of supplies in the Northwest. Even by 1986, the southeastern United States was supplying 47 percent of the nation's timber harvest, compared with 25 percent in the Pacific Northwest (Postel and Ryan 1991). The markets of the Pacific Rim also have reached there: South Korea's Donghae Paper Company has been among the corporations seeking to open chipping mills in Alabama and Tennessee.

Less well known is the growing importance of Chile as a source of wood for the Pacific Rim. By 1989 the Chilean timber industry was already exporting to five major wood-consuming countries: West Germany,

Belgium, Brazil, the United States, and Japan, with one-quarter of the exports going to Japan (Hagler 1993). Along with the United States, Australia, and Canada, Chile now accounts for 87 percent of fiber exports to Japan (Dudley 1992). Chilean wood exports have more than doubled since 1983 (Postel and Ryan 1991).

As part of a general push to increase its pulp and paper capacity, Chile has accelerated the conversion of its millennia-old native *alerce* forests to monoculture plantations slated for chipping and export. By 1991, Chile had planted 1.3 million acres of plantations, 85 percent of which contained just one species, the introduced Monterey Pine.

Boreal Forests

The boreal taiga of Siberia and the Russian Far East is considered the "ultimate wild card" in predictions of growth in timber supply in both the Pacific Rim and global markets (Hagler 1993). With the collapse of the centralized Soviet system, local and regional governments have attempted to assert control over natural resources. Timber "mafias" also have come to power, especially in the Far East. Attempts by multinational giants like Weyerhauser and Georgia-Pacific to set up joint ventures have been stalled by political and economic chaos.

Regional governments increasingly have become suspicious of foreign firms. South Korea's Hyundai Corporation has been restricted from logging any more of the Bikin River basin north of Vladivostok. A large-scale joint venture with Japan also has been slowed by fluctuations in supplies and high prices charged by Siberian partners. The nearness of the huge Asian markets of Japan, Taiwan, and South Korea virtually ensures that exports of Siberian timber will increase in the future. A major market for Siberian wood exists just across the border.

The Question of China

Just as Siberia figures prominently in projections of timber supply in the Pacific Rim and beyond, China is becoming a major factor in terms of demand for wood products. Rapid economic growth and overcutting of domestic forests have brought about an acute timber shortage. The economic reforms of the late 1970s led to a jump in demand for wood. Annual harvests almost doubled from 1976 to 1988, and the area of timber-producing forests has shrunk by almost 3 million hectares since 1980 (Postel and Ryan 1991).

At the current rate of consumption, China will have harvested all of its remaining productive forests within a decade, and imports can be expected to rise substantially well before that. China has already become the major importer of plywood from Indonesia (Graham 1993). The government has set a goal of planting 30 million hectares of trees by the year 2000 and has planted an estimated 10 million hectares of plantations in the expectation of doubling domestic wood production (Postel and Ryan 1991).

Shape of the Global Timber Trade: "Institutional Arrangements"

The fragmentation of the Siberian timber industry is a notable exception to the prevailing trends of increased integration and centralization in the global timber industry. An examination of the Pacific Rim timber trade shows two central characteristics: first, all of its forests, whatever their type and location, are tied into one market; and second, that market continues to be basically colonial in character, with centers of demand drawing upon distant sources of supply.

This colonial model of resource use also has shaped what might be called the "institutional arrangements" by which the timber trade has worked with governments to ensure access to wood supplies. In the tropical countries, timber barons often control logging concessions and revenues from export. But "institutional arrangements" are not limited to third world countries. Canada's liquidation of its forests has followed the colonial model as well.

Forest destruction in Canada has proceeded through a provincial tenure system that grants logging companies huge concessions on public lands at bargain prices which include some of the lowest stumpage fees in the world. Homegrown timber giant MacMillan Bloedel has been given generous terms for logging British Columbia. In Alberta, Mitsubishi Corporation has been allowed to lease an area the size of Ohio to feed its pulp operations, and Daishowa Pulp Company has built the world's largest disposable wooden chopstick factory among old-growth aspen forests (McInnis 1994a).

When Daishowa Corporation's Peace River Pulp Company built a $579 million mill in Alberta in 1988, approximately $70 million of the infrastructure costs were borne by the taxpayers. Similarly, Alberta-Pacific Company, 85 percent Japanese-owned, finished construction of the world's largest bleached kraft pulp mill near Athabasca in 1993 with the province paying infrastructure costs of $75 million and with an agreement that the company need not begin repayment until the mill becomes profitable (McInnis 1994a).

This kind of arrangement means that the government is in effect a shareholder in such operations, even though their terms are not voted on by citizens. In British Columbia, the government was until recently an actual shareholder in MacMillan Bloedel, to whom it awarded the largest number of timber concessions. The Canadian taxpayers thus have ended up paying the economic as well as environmental costs of a volatile market: the combination of an oversupply of pulp and intense international competition has led the pulp industry in Canada to lose more than $1 billion in the last three years (McInnis 1994b). The vicissitudes of the wood fiber market have also resulted in longer-term strategies on the part of importers. Japan relies on Australia for over one-third of its imports of wood chips (Graham 1993). This stems from two "chip scares" in 1980 and 1987, which led Japan to broaden its sources of supply (Hagler 1993). Softwood chip prices doubled overnight in 1980, and Japanese importers found themselves completely dependent on U.S. West Coast exporters, with no other sources of supply. After suffering significant losses, they diversified their supply sources by importing from Australia. When Australian supplies of eucalyptus chips were threatened by a proposed pulp mill in 1987, Japan turned to southeastern U.S. suppliers.

While the evolution of the Pacific Rim and global timber trades has proceeded by a combination of accident and design, the second element has been the stronger. Given the shape of the market now—the increased emphasis on pulp and paper, the ability to use many different kinds of wood from a variety of regions, and the ever-growing demand in established and emerging economies—this element of design carries the most serious implications for the survival of native forests. Without changes in national and global policy, temperate forests will be depleted in a manner similar to the way the tropical forests have been, and the industry will move into Siberia in a big way.

Missing from market projections, however, is any accounting for social and environmental consequences. The fact that northern forests are thought to represent a major "carbon pool" which helps to regulate earth's climate, and that widespread depletion of the taiga could accelerate the process of global warming, is only the most dramatic consequence (Rosencranz and Scott 1992).

Equally striking is the fact that industrial logging usually is subsidized to varying degrees by governments of lands possessing timber supplies. The very volatility of the wood products market makes generous institutional arrangements with compliant governments a virtual necessity for the timber industry. As Alistair Graham (1993) puts it, "Despite all this fawning to international capital at the expense of our democracy and native forests, [the industry] still cannot get a competitive investment unless governments come to the party with large chunks of cash—infrastructure support, tax holidays, royalty discounts, and accelerated depreciation perks—and so spread the costs across the whole community."

Aside from specific instances of bribery and collusion (which are not uncommon), the motivation of governments to participate in such arrangements may seem unclear. John McInnis (1994a) of the Western Canada Wilderness Committee has framed the basic question: "We should ask why governments are so eager to subsidize the production of more pulp, the liquidation of more taiga resources, more pollution, more incursion into aboriginal homelands." The answer lies partly in a flawed system of valuing forests and quantifying the costs of their destruction that informs the decision-making process in most governments.

Toward a Solution: Revaluing Forests

The natural resources accounting systems traditionally used by governments tend to favor industrial logging and forest liquidation (World Resources Institute 1992–93, 1994–95). On the national level, natural resource accounting policies encourage forest destruction and degradation by *under*valuing forests that are intact. "Value" is typically seen in terms of value as timber. Nontimber goods usually are ignored in economic assessments of forests because they lack conventional commodity value. Yet these very goods—including environmental services (soil conservation, water cleansing, carbon storage), fruits, resins, and oils—often have an economic value that exceeds that of timber. What they lack is the infrastructure support that makes industrial logging possible.

Undervaluing the forest ecosystem goes hand in hand with *over*estimating the economic benefits, both current and projected, of timber harvesting and forest conversion. The benefits of logging are usually calculated without taking into account the environmental and social costs of deforestation. These may be hard to quantify, but the World Resources Institute (1992–93, 1994–95) and a growing number of economists have shown that if just the costs of infrastructure, tax credits, and production subsidies are added in accounts of forest revenues, the anticipated economic benefits of forest conversion may vanish.

The social costs of deforestation also are substantial. In many countries, both forestry laws and indigenous rights and claims routinely are ignored. The effects on tribal peoples have been overwhelmingly negative, especially in tropical countries experiencing rapid population growth. Ecological disaster usually means social disaster, as in the Philippines, where denuded hillsides caused mudslides that killed thousands after extensive flooding. In the United States and Canada, rural employment generated by logging has been manipulated as a political issue, but as indicated above, the industry itself has been eliminating jobs steadily through greater automation in both mills and harvesting technology, and through the export of both raw or minimally processed logs and chips. Industrial logging also ties rural communities to a "boom or bust" economic structure, which decreases economic and thus social stability.

In Canada, the tropics, Siberia, and many national forests in the United States (such as Alaska's Tongass), royalties and taxes from timber concessions also tend to be set at unrealistically low rates. Government revenues are thus only a fraction of what they could be. Subsidies for harvesting and processing compound the loss of timber revenues for national and local governments. Undervaluing the resource thus encourages overuse and depletion.

Correcting this flawed accounting system is fairly straightforward in theory: forest resources need a revaluation that reflects the full costs of their loss. Forest resources and the environmental as well as economic services that they provide have to be seen as capital assets *before* timber harvest, assets whose depreciation has to be incorporated into any adequate accounting system (World Resources Institute 1992–93, 1994–95). In the model proposed by the World Resources Institute, national budgets that strive to incorporate the full value of forests to a country's well-being would eliminate or reduce most timber subsidies. They want to charge logging prices that reflect environmental and social costs of harvests *and* reward sustainable harvest practices through the kind of incentives now available to standard industrial logging.

The Global Imperative

All national reforms, of course, must contend with the size, scope, and momentum of a global timber trade, which has tied all of the world's forests into one market. Not only does demand rise and fall on a global level, but the very structures of economic development are tied to the market: per capita consumption of paper is a central indicator of the level of development. Alistair Graham (1993) paints a grim picture: "Present levels of, and rates of growth of, demand for wood products are so high that the chances of protecting large areas of remaining native forests of high conservation value are low unless major product substitution takes place, demand for virgin fibre is suppressed as much as possible, and rigorous conservation policies are put in place by countries and corporations alike and all very quickly indeed."

Institutional tools for dealing with this situation appear limited. The record of international bodies such as the International Tropical Timber Organization and the U.N. Commission on Sustainable Development in modifying global timber practices is extremely uneven. The scope for national action has become more uncertain with the passage of the Uruguay Round of the General Agreement on Tariffs and Trade (GATT), which directly affects the ability of a country to restrict the flow of natural resources in and out of its borders. The Uruguay Round also could complicate the implementation of key international reforms such as a global system of wood certification based on economic and environmental sustainability.

The most potent tools available for reducing the consumption of and the demand for wood products are found in consumer-driven "demand management" strategies. The minimum recycled-content laws and requirements put in place on both the state and federal levels in the United States have led to a rapid jump in the use, demand, and price of recycled paper. The use of "tree-free" paper made from kenaf and hemp also has had an impact on the wood products market.

Conclusion

The global forest crisis is tied directly to the evolution of a global market for wood products and the internationalization of the timber industry. There are pervasive ethical issues related to these structures: institutional arrangements between governments and industry facilitate industrial logging and exploitation of public lands, and governments tend to rely on flawed accounting systems that undervalue forests and their benefits. These structures also operate in the context of an irreplaceable loss of biodiversity and ecosystems and harmful impacts on local and indigenous communities. In the face of institutional inadequacy for addressing the scope and severity of the problem, consumer-driven demand management strategies involving recycling and alternate fiber materials appear to be the most effective means at hand for catalyzing change on a significant level.

REFERENCES

Dudley, Nigel. 1992. *Forests in Trouble: A Review of the Status of Forests Worldwide.* Gland, Switzerland: World Wildlife Fund.

Graham, Alistair. 1993. "Wood Flows around the Pacific Rim: A Corporate Picture." *Forestry, Pulp, and Paper,* June.

Hagler, Robert. 1993. "Global Forest." *Papermaker,* May.

McInnis, John. 1994a. "The Great Alberta Giveaway: The Japanese Connection." *Taiga News,* no. 9 (May).

———. 1994b. "Mitsubishi in Canada: The Fiasco Continues." *World Rain Forest Report* 11 (January–March).

Nectoux, François, and Yoichi Kuroda. 1989. "Timber from the South Seas: An Analysis of Japan's Tropical Timber Trade and Its Environmental Impact." *World Wildlife International.* Tokyo: Tsukiji Shokan.

Postel, Sandra, and John Ryan. 1991. "Reforming Forestry." In *State of the World 1991,* ed. Worldwatch Institute, 74–92. New York: W. W. Norton.

Rosencranz, Armin, and Antony Scott. 1992. "Siberia's Threatened Forests." *Nature,* January 23.

"Eight Years Left for the Solomon Islands." 1994. *World Rain Forest Report* 11 (July–September).

World Resources Institute. 1992–93. "Forests and Rangelands." *World Resources Institute: Guide to the Global Environment.* New York: Oxford University Press.

———. 1994–95. "Forests and Rangelands." *World Resources Institute: Guide to the Global Environment.* New York: Oxford University Press.

ALBERT F. IKE & DORINDA G. DALLMEYER

Where Do We Go from Here?

To have an impact, environmental ethics must move beyond academic discussion and into the policy arena to deal with global environmental conflicts including first world versus third world, consumption versus conservation, and the needs of transitional economies versus environmental protection. At the outset, we need a theoretical basis for an ethical framework that incorporates social costs and benefits. Simultaneously, we need to ensure that our dialogue explores assumptions of all sides entering the discourse.

We need to examine what "justice" should mean, especially cross-culturally, between north and south. Is there some root meaning we can agree on? Does it apply in principle? Can the marketplace be used to achieve it?

We need to look more carefully at relations between poverty and environmentalism and at justice concerns between rich and poor. This means taking economics seriously. In addition to exploring problems caused by steep economic gradients, intergenerational equity should be evaluated for its utility for consciousness-raising within the business and consumers' communities.

With a full understanding of economic and social justice issues, we can begin to develop a framework for making explicit the implicit ethics and values that control our approach. Promoting a healthy environment requires a clear understanding of its value, where this attribution of value is epistemologically grounded in a solid foundation. General acceptance of ethical norms depends, in the long run, on those norms being justified in a convincing way. For this reason, true progress in the fight to save the environment cannot be achieved until a philosophically acceptable theoretical framework for environmental ethics and the implications of that framework are worked out. The framework must be acceptable to business and scientifically minded people. There does not have to be a complete consensus on the philosophical foundations, but some frameworks are clearly on stronger epistemological footing than others. If business people and citizens in general are to be convinced of the importance of environmental issues, we must rely primarily on these sturdier foundations to achieve that goal.

Concern over the impact of economic and business practices must be limited to the pursuit of "the good" based on the value system of a society which not only reflects short-term benefits and costs but also respects future generations and the interconnectedness of humans with the life systems that compose nature.

Ethics implies intrinsic or inherent valuation, not simply instrumental valuation typical of an economic perspective. We need to move to a new metaphysics of nature to underlie the ethics. Until we do this, we are trapped by top-down anthropocentrism/anthropomorphism. In other words, nature must be recognized as having intrinsic value, not simply— or only—its resource value. We need to create a philosophical framework for environmental ethics that addresses methodology and metaphysical foundations while making people aware of conflicting models in environmental philosophy.

For the future, we should emphasize the adoption of an interdisciplinary approach in policy making. Decisions should include and/or be based on ethical considerations, and goals made accordingly, but economic considerations must play a role in achieving these goals as efficiently as possible. We need to emphasize further attention to true interdisciplinarity, as opposed to multidisciplinarity, as well as further attention to notions of system holism.

Environmental concerns, which reflect the interconnection of production, distribution, and consumption practices with environmental impacts, must be seen as inherent and vital to economic and business decisions and be made part of the financial dynamic and policy processes.

Corporate representatives, academics, and public policymakers must be involved in the process of redefining a sustainable society, which we realize may be a long-term effort. To achieve any results whatsoever, we must maintain honest and open communication among ethicists, business leaders, policymakers, economists, and others.

Historically, business has been a mechanistic construct focusing on wealth generation while avoiding those costs or negative outcomes that can be "charged" to others or be subsidized by the general public. Economics should (as has been its role) seek to allocate resources to achieve these goals efficiently. It should, however, take proper valuation of environmental goods into consideration. It remains to be seen if corporate "business as usual" can be reformed to be ecofriendly. Perhaps business itself must change into another form.

What are the social costs and benefits of linking values and ethical concerns into policy issues? We need to explore mechanisms and strategies for systematically linking values and ethical concerns to policy (context, problems, potentials). Ethics, which is an intrinsic valuation process, must become an integral part of policy making. Business and political leaders should facilitate the incorporation of environmental ethics into decision making at the local, regional, and international levels. Otherwise, future decisions will be formulated much as past decisions have been, and the environment will be treated, again, much as it has been in the past.

We have a responsibility to make practical, implementable recommendations to put principles into action. One method may be to look at case studies to reveal the "realities" that impede or promote subsequent integration. We need to offer ways of establishing linkages systematically to bring ethics into the policy process, such as involving environmental ethicists more often in public policy formation. By using that method, it would be possible to move environmental ethics and the positions generated from academic venues into the congressional and international arena. This movement may require nongovernmental organizations, rather than elected officials, to lay the groundwork.

How can we change incentive/disincentive structures to level the playing field between economics and environment? To achieve a comprehensive inclusion of ethics into policy and practice, we need to provide attractive incentives for business to adopt environmentally sound practices. These should include profit incentives as well as attempts to change fundamental values. What is the logic of ethically constrained behavior for companies? We know this well from personal behavior; for example, we choose to borrow money rather than to steal it. The challenge is to develop a model of ethically constrained profit maximization.

In addition to efforts to reform the system, those who are truly interested in incorporating ethics and values into how we organize ourselves first should try to apply to their own lives what they would like to see businesses do. Once we have been able to order our own lives, then there is the possibility that we can make meaningful contributions in the wider sphere.

Contributors

JAN WILLEM BOL, a native of the Netherlands, is now a farmer in Wisconsin after a varied career in both academe and the business world. He has taught marketing at Miami University, Oxford, Ohio, and he has also been a visiting professor at the Institute for Environmental Studies at the University of Wisconsin–Madison. Dr. Bol previously served as partner and vice president of corporate research and development at Burke Marketing Services.

TERENCE J. CENTNER is a professor with the University of Georgia College of Agricultural and Environmental Sciences, Athens. He received a B.S. (with distinction) in agriculture from Cornell University, a J.D. from the State University of New York at Buffalo, and an LL.M. in agricultural law from the University of Arkansas. Centner's research program involves the policy analysis of environmental and agricultural legislation, the fusion of economic theory with law applied to specific problems, and the development of new regulatory institutions to respond to market imperfections.

DOUG DAIGLE, an environmental advocate and educator, has an M.A. in environmental ethics from Colorado State University. He directed the global environmental education program for the Pacific Environment and Resources Center in California, which focused on environmental trends in the Pacific Rim. Daigle is program director for the Coalition to Restore Coastal Louisiana. His research includes environmental impacts of the global timber trade, environmental economics, and the ethical and environmental aspects of climate change.

DORINDA G. DALLMEYER has been research director of the Dean Rusk Center for International and Comparative Law since 1984. Before earning a J.D. degree at the University of Georgia, she conducted research in tropical marine biology and ecology. The editor of a book on rights to oceanic resources, she helped the International Environment Institute draft an international agreement on transboundary marine pollution. A faculty member of the Environmental Ethics Certificate Program, she teaches seminars on law and diplomacy and on environmental dispute resolution.

FREDERICK FERRÉ is research professor of philosophy and cofounder of the Environmental Ethics Certificate Program at the University of Georgia. He served for eight years as general editor of *Research in Philosophy and Technology*. He is known within his discipline for his writings on religion, science, technology, and the environment. He has degrees from Boston University, Vanderbilt, and St. Andrews in Scotland, and he taught at Vanderbilt, Mount Holyoke, and Dickinson before joining the faculty at Georgia.

EUGENE HARGROVE is chair of the Department of Philosophy and Religion Studies at the University of North Texas, where he runs an M.A. program in philosophy with a concentration in environmental ethics. He is founding editor of the journal *Environmental Ethics,* author of *Foundations of Environmental Ethics* (Prentice Hall), and editor of a number of books, most recently *The Animal Rights/Environmental Ethics Debate: The Environmental Perspective* (SUNY).

ALBERT F. IKE is chairman of the faculty of the Environmental Ethics Certificate Program and associate vice president for public service and outreach at the University of Georgia. He holds degrees from Rutgers, Cornell, and North Carolina State. His academic training was in forestry and soil science, but most of his work for the past twenty years has been in the area of administration. His areas of interest are land use, regional planning, and coastal zone management.

WARREN KRIESEL is an associate professor in the Agricultural and Applied Economics Department at the University of Georgia. Following service in the Peace Corps, he earned advanced degrees at Virginia Tech and Ohio State University. Dr. Kriesel teaches rural economic development and econometrics, and his research interests include natural resource economics, industrial location, and educational finance.

WILLIAM J. MCKINNEY is associate professor and chair of the Department of Philosophy and Religion at Southeast Missouri State University in Cape Girardeau, where he teaches courses in scientific reasoning, environmental ethics, and advanced symbolic logic. His research interests involve studies of the intersection of the philosophies of science and technology with environmental ethics, epistemic problems of experimental science, and computer-assisted instruction in the sciences and the philosophy of science. He holds degrees from Bucknell and Indiana Universities.

JUDITH L. MEYER, research professor in the Institute of Ecology at the University of Georgia, teaches courses in environmental literacy and aquatic ecology. She has degrees from Michigan, Hawaii, and Cornell. Her research on stream ecosystems focuses on the role of microbes in stream food webs. A former president of the Ecological Society of America, she is a fellow of the American Association for the Advancement of Science, and she has served on the Water Science and Technology Board of the National Research Council/National Academy of Sciences.

MARKKU OKSANEN from the Department of Philosophy at the University of Turku, Finland, completed his licentiate's degree in 1992 and expects to receive his doctorate in 1998. His dissertation is *Nature as Property? Environmental Ethics and the Institution of Ownership*. He has done postgraduate work at the University of Wales, College of Cardiff, and has published articles and book reviews on environmental and political philosophy. He is coeditor of the anthology *Environmental Philosophy: Essays on the Ethics of Environmental Protection* [in Finnish].

MARK SAGOFF is senior research scholar at the Institute for Philosophy and Public Policy at the University of Maryland, where he served as director from 1989 to 1996. He has degrees from Harvard, Columbia, and the University of Rochester. He has published in scholarly journals of philosophy, law, and economics and in popular periodicals. His book, *The Economy of the Earth: Philosophy, Law, and the Environment*, was published in 1988 by Cambridge University Press. He was selected in 1991 as a Pew Charitable Trust Scholar in Conservation and the Environment.

DAVID SKRBINA is deputy director of the Eco-Philosophy Center in Ann Arbor, Michigan. He also works as an engineering manager at Ford Motor Company and is an adjunct faculty member in the Department of Mathematics at the University of Michigan–Dearborn. He has master's degrees in applied mathematics and electrical engineering from the University of Michigan and was recently admitted to the Ph.D. program at the University of Bath (England) School of Management.

THADDEUS C. TRZYNA, chairman emeritus of the IUCN Commission on Environmental Strategy and Planning, is president of the California Institute of Public Affairs and senior associate at the Center for Politics and Economics,

Claremont Graduate University. His areas of interest include environmental policy, international development, and decision making.

ANDREW YOUNG, former ambassador to the United Nations in the Carter administration, now serves as cochairman of GoodWorks International, an Atlanta-based consulting group that provides strategic services to corporations and governments operating in the global economy. He served three terms in the U.S. House of Representatives and was elected to two terms as mayor of Atlanta. He serves on the board of directors of several corporations, including Delta Airlines, Argus, Archer Daniels Midland, Cox Communications, and Thomas Nelson Publishing. His awards include the Presidential Medal of Freedom, Legion d'Honneur, and more than forty-five honorary degrees from such universities as Yale, Notre Dame, Emory, and the University of Georgia.

Index